1

Manhattan New York is a world attraction, hands down. A true landmark and symbol of American freedom by day, and a glamorizing light show under the night skies. It's no wonder people from all over the world move and live here despite the sky-high rent with nothing included, or the many dangers that come with choosing such a large and exposed city.

    With the many dangers of shootings, muggings, and other things that happen to people who are even minding their own business, the police provide good protection. They are some of the bravest and boldest of the big city. Well, any city for that matter. Most cops do well answering the call of duty, and some go the extra mile. Isn't prevention the best medicine? Well that is exactly what one little young Lady name Anna does. Her name is Anna Davis, and she works for the D District at Manhattan South. Three years on the force, and she's still not one of those asshole cops who's only interest in life is to put other's behind bars, nor plague those poor new drivers with a rain of parking tickets. Of course she would if she had to, but for the most part her heart was almost as beautiful as her looks. She had a strong and sincere belief in helping people. Half of the people that she arrested were given huge breaks on the evidence and charges before she turned them in to the station. Now if that's not a look out I don't know what is.

Like most people she had one flaw, a short temper, and in that state of mind she tackled the big boys with no fear or thought of losing. I mean without back up. She had even earned a nickname: Sister Davis. Ok like I said, she was beautiful. She was slender build, stood 5 foot 6, long black hair with body and tan smooth skin. Many would say that she had no business being a cop but she was good at what she did and was stronger than you might think, very smart and respected by all. She works the night shift from 11pm to 7am, or as they call it, 21 hundred hours to zero 7 hundred. On this shift Officer Davis would patrol the streets and make sure that they were safe. She also responded to the normal night shift calls such as break-ins, robberies, shootings, drunk and unruly people, and other disputes.

The reason why she joined the force was because she wanted to be involved in the committee, and make a positive difference. If she saw someone who was doing something that they weren't supposed to be doing, such as public intoxication, graffiti, or fighting, she would usually just correct them and send them on their way. But if she had seen someone doing anything more serious than that, they were most likely going to get arrested. Anna is a person who understands that it is not always about taking people off of the street. Some people just need guidance, and there were times that she found herself playing the role of a consoler and a friend. That is how this officer earned her respect; while many others were only feared.

However, in the events that she had to catch fleeing suspects, she may not have been as strong as the guys, but her agility put most men on the force to shame. There were times when young fleeing suspects ran through allies, and hopped tall fences, ran up the stairs of New York City buildings and jumped from roof-top to roof-top in order to escape. Most of her backup could not keep up and were forced to give up the chase, or slow down to a walk. But Anna stayed hot on their trail until she had caught them. Then her backup came, either out of breath, or slowly climbing over a fence, or standing at one building while getting ready to come over there to her taking the long way. Yet with all her training and moderate experience, as well as some gifted and developed skills, nothing but nothing, could prepare her for tonight.

October15th 2010 1:18 a.m. as Anna drove on patrol she noticed two people in an alley in a scuffle somewhere between 9th and 10th street. She had a feeling that something wasn't right so she flashed her light and siren and the man dropped his arms. A lady was holding him, perhaps his girlfriend. Anna was relieved, just a silly couple fooling around. It's late and she didn't feel like telling them to get a room or take it home. Ms Davis has not the care or the time for this so starts to pulls off and goes on her merry way until the girlfriend drops her boyfriend and starts for the shadows of the alley.

"Hey! Hey you come here!"

The young woman started to run into the dark alley of 9th street.

Anna darts after the woman without hesitation, Maglite in hand, and radios her position as she runs up to the man.

"It looks like a man has been stabbed. I need some back up and a paramedic in the alley of 9th street in-between 1st and 2nd avenue. I need a paramedic immediately!"

"Roger that unit 43, right away!"

"I'm going after the suspect, she's running through the alley headed towards 8th street."

"No go 43, Wait for backup"

"She's getting away I have to catch her"

Anna is determined to catch the female suspect, she

chased straight behind her into the night while yelling at her, warning that she's a police officer and that she needs to stop. The lady ignoring her, runs and hops a very tall gate with ease, and mistakenly believed that she had a little more time to make the getaway. But to her surprise Anna was right behind her. She used the tic-tac method (that she learned from watching Jackie Chan movies) to quickly hop the fence before tackling her. This pissed her off greatly, she through Anna off of her then started to walk toward her. There was no way Anna was going to let this women near her again. If she had kill a man, then nearly jumped straight over the fence, then through her off like a small pet, then she is surely more dangerous then she expected. Anna took out her gun a warned her to stay back, but the lady didn't listen, instead she came closer, perhaps to take the weapon and disarm her. Anna felted that she had no choice but to shoot. She shot her in the abdomen once with her pistol. The lady screamed but did not go down, so Anna shot her again, this time in the chest. She still didn't go down.

"Aah! Bitch if you shoot me again I will take that gun and

shove it down your throat!"

Now Anna is stunned and doesn't know what to think or what to do. Two shots to the body, you would think she would be on the ground or barely moving, or not moving at all for that matter. She thinks to herself that maybe, just maybe, she should just let that crazy heifer go. She backs up while shaking her head wondering how this lady is still able to stand.

The suspect is in rage and is not in the mood for any apologies or compromise. The woman acts like she is going rush at her. This must be some kind of rage blackout or drug or something. Anna wanted the girl in custody, not dead. Perhaps that guy tried to rape her and she lost her ever beloved mind. She's not looking very happy and that would explain a lot. Even if this is true how is she still standing? Anna just hopes that this woman doesn't think she's going to stab her too. No sir, she better get that out her head. It appears that on a normal day she would be a pretty nice girl, well except for now. She tries to get at Anna again, opening her mouth, perhaps trying to tell her something. The lady approaches Anna and opens her mouth wide, and it looks like Cujo!!

Anna, scared out of her mind for the first time since her childhood bogeyman, loses all her cool while screaming, points the gun a little higher and goes for the head shots. "Pop! Pop!"

The suspect falls backwards and hits the ground like a ton of bricks. Anna can't even think to calm down before a man comes up behind her from the dark and takes the gun out of her hand. He took the gun from her so easily that it appeared as if she just handed it over. He's very upset, huffing and puffing.

"You stupid girl" he yells angrily. "What did you do? Why did you do that?"

Anna witnessed the man's transformation as he angrily yells at her. Boy these people sure can get ugly, almost beast like. Are they even human? The only two things that Anna knew for sure were that her life was in danger, and the man now has her gun. This actually means three, once again, her life is now positively in danger.

" I'm sorry, I didn't mean to… umm wait right here"

Anna bolts back, turns around and starts to run through the alley in a feeble attempt to get away, but another female slightly older serves her with the meanest knuckle sandwich she ever felt. Anna is knocked out but not cold, she's just in a daze and can't get up. She can only see in a blur and hear in a slur as the other female and male speak.

"Carol is Donna ok?"

"Yeah she'll be fine James. Next time you need to do a better job at training."

"I know, I turned her, but this is only her second night out. Give her a little slack"

"Fine but kill the mortal. Donna needs another snack"

James walks over to Donna and the policewoman. Anna gets up and runs back toward the police car.

"J feed Donna, I will deal with that run-away meal"

She goes after Anna and catches her. Determination and fear drives Anna to be strong and plenty resourceful as she knees Carol in the stomach, then swings her flashlight and beats Carol with it repeatedly. Flashlight and feet, a wicked sight to see, then she tries to run again before realizing that she is running the wrong way, her police car is on 9th and she was running toward 8th. So she turned around and ran right towards James. This surprised him as he tries to catch her, but she jukes him and then used the same tic-tac method to hop back over the gate. The tables had turned, and now it is she, who is on the run.

James is right behind her across the gate, in which appeared to be in a single leap before he catches up and grabs her. He bites her from behind on the neck. She feels the sharp teeth then the blood rushing out of her. That's it she's going to die, she is going to die, here in this alley. No! Not tonight! She sticks her fingers in both of his eyes and he lets go. She maces him using the whole can of pepper spray and manages to escape into the car where she pulled off wildly, petal to the metal. Anna Made it two blocks before she starts feeling faint, and that is what she does. Hits a bus stop shelter and the telephone booth next to it; she did this right in front of her arriving backup.

On that street corner there was shattered glass, quarters, and confused cops everywhere. This is one fine mess out here.

"I don't know what's going on but we have an officer down! Officer down! Call the paramedic and proceed with caution! " The sergeant screamed into the radio as the other cops scattered and took cover behind the cars guns drawn. They asked, "Who? Who caused this?" Officer Davis reported only one suspect and it was a woman whom was possibly armed only with a knife. Did someone open fire on car # 43 causing her to crash, or did some ballsy reckless kid steal her car and lost control? Nope, it's definitely her and she's bleeding from the neck. Just as officer Grey suspected, one of his officers are down.

Detective Kyle Miller, a personal friend of Anna, not an old friend but a friend indeed rips off his sleeve and applies pressure to the wound until the ambulance shows. As they lay her on the bed and carry her inside, Miller climbs up to aid at her side. "Sorry detective. We believe you should stay back at this time."

"But I know her; she would want me to come."

"Sorry but we don't know this sir, if you would please."

Anna comes to. Just barely enough to recognize what was going on and who was there, and she grabs the Detective's hand then passes back out.

"Ok sir I guess you were right, you can come but please let us do our jobs."

On the way to the hospital, as they are giving her plasma, she wakes up again and calmly looks around.

"Anna are you ok? What happened back there?"

She tells him. She tells him everything: about the girl, about the guy in the alley and how She chased her down and shot her in once in the abdomen, once in the chest, and how young woman just kept on coming, and how she was forced to shot her twice in the head.

"But Anna you know you can't do all that it's too much."

She explained that she didn't want to kill that blond girl, but she left her no choice. There was also a man. He stanched the gun away from her and screamed at her as if she was his child. She didn't know if he was going to hurt her and wasn't sticking around to find out. She started to run, but she

didn't make three steps before she had a rather rude

meeting with another woman.

"So that explains the black eye? You sure it wasn't the guy?

"No, it was the other girl."

Anna describes all three as Caucasian starting with the man.

She describes the man as being tall and muscular, dark

brown hair and decently dressed. Nice blue blazer and black

slacks. The woman who floored her was slightly older, brown

skirt and black hair. Oh, and boy did Anna hate to admit that

she was pretty. Secretly she is hoping that the tune up she

gave the other woman did a little makeover, and then she

becomes instantly ashamed when she tells him.

"I don't want to be like that Kyle. Does that make me a bad

person?"

"No, I don't think that makes you a bad person at all. You

did what you had to do to get out of there. Also you said the

guy bit you?"

"Yes he did, but I got away. I'm pretty sure he's hurt too,

they should still be there or close by."

"Ok that should at least shed a little more light on everything that happened here and why. Not to mention putting these hoodlums or crazed people who ever they are behind bars."

"Kyle?"

"Yes Ms. Davis?"

He calls her Ms. Davis to show her a more personal bond. She told him a long time ago that she would like him to call her Anna, or Ms. Davis when they were off duty, all of her close friends and old friends, and even family were already use to doing this.

"I know this is a long stretch but…"

"I'm listening, go on"

"I think they were vampires"

"Vampires? I see. Get some rest dear you've had a long night."

Anna didn't bother talking about it for the rest of that night. She knew what Miller was really thinking. No she didn't lose her mind out there. Still that story was hard to believe and even she knew it. She felt alone. Not that her colleagues wouldn't be there to protect her, but if they don't even believe her how can they protect her or even themselves? The other police checked out the alley. They found the man who was killed. Then they found a puddle of blood back in the deep alley by the gate.

So the morning news in the papers went like this: "MAN STABBED TO DEATH; OFFICER ASSAULTED," "THREE SOUGHT IN KILLING, POLICE AMBUSH," "COP KILLER GANG MARAUDING ALPHABET CITY," A man was stabbed to death last night in an alley off Ninth Street, near Avenue C, and a police officer responding was assaulted and stabbed after shooting and wounding a female suspect. Officer Anna Davis barely escaped with her own life as she was brutally beaten and stabbed in the neck by a group of unknown people aiding the murder suspect. The suspect remains at large and has been injured, police say, with 2 bullet wounds in the torso. She is described as being 5'7" or 5'8", with blond hair and was last seen wearing blue jeans and a pink sports bra. Two other suspects are described as…

It is 8:00 in the morning. As Anna is reading this she gets an uncomfortable feeling that this isn't over by far, and even worse than that she feels like she's in the twilight zone. Still, despite her intuition maybe this whole thing will blow over in a couple of days. New York has five boroughs and something is happing every night in each one. She puts down the paper then rolls over and goes back to sleep. An hour later she receives a phone call.

"Pumpkin are you alright?"

"Daddy?"

"Yeah sweetheart it's me, your mother heard about you, ok we read about what happened to you in the paper. Hold on your mother wants to talk to you."

"Sweetie we were worried sick about you. You have to be more careful."

"Yeah Pumpkin please don't chase any more people though those alleys ever. Let the men do that stuff, back up or not. Do you understand me young lady?"

"Yes Daddy, it won't happen again."

"Yeah sweetie, I have to agree with your father. Were just

glad you're okay after that stabbing."

"Mom if I tell you something will you promise not to laugh or dismiss what I tell you?"

"You know you can tell us anything. What's wrong? Is someone threatening you?"

"No mom it's about those people whom I encountered in the alley, I think they're vampires."

"Yeah you mean people who sleep all day and up all night like vampires?"

"No I mean real vampires, there were three of them. I shot one of them four times but it doesn't matter, she must have still made it home. The other girl I beat with a flashlight and she got back up. The guy bit me and…"

"Real vampires you say?"

"Pumpkin, I think that you had a rough night."

"You said that you weren't going to…"

"It wasn't me Anna dear it was your father. Donald I'm worried about Anna. I think she's delirious"

"This is your fault Carrie, you shouldn't have let her watch all those scary movies."

"Ok mom, dad, I'm right here and I can hear you. Plus I'm the one who's supposed to be freaking out right now."

"Sweetie we're coming to see you."

"Mom where are y'all right now anyway?"

"Pumpkin me and your mother are right down stairs, but this bonehead security guard won't let us up."

"Why didn't you guys tell me you were already here? Here I come."

She got up out of bed and dashed out of her room. The nurse asked her where she was off to. When Anna explained to her that her parents were down stairs and she was going down to get them, the nurse made the phone call to tell security to let the parents up to see her.

After her parents leave she is glad and grateful but a little annoyed. Annoyed all over again that she opened her mouth again about last night, but at least she's a lot less scared.

At lunch time the nurse serves Anna her meal, and she tries to eat it, boy does she try and boy is she hungry. Nonetheless, her throat closes up after the first bite. What the hey! What the heck. It must be some kind of flu or something this is ridiculous. This can't be happening! Could it be lockjaw?

When she finally catches her breath she feels a sharp sense of anger mixed with confusion. Anna puts the pillow over her face and screams at the top of her lungs. Well one thing is for sure, she doesn't have lockjaw. Maybe it's the mumps or even the damn chickenpox. Anna is getting angrier and angrier until she feels her forehead crinkle. All she knows for sure is that she is going to kill that pig of a man that did this to her, and maybe she ought to leave the hospital and look for him before the doctor tells her something that would absolutely crush her. Maybe it would be a good idea to get laid tonight; it would make her happier and much calmer. She smiles at the idea. No! Wait hell no. How selfish and evil. Not until the doctor gives good news. Even with condoms it wouldn't be right or fair until she hears that she's in good health and doesn't have anything.

"Ah, I'm going to kill that pig of a man!"

Anna doesn't notice that the nurse has already opened the door and walked in to check on Anna and take her tray.

"Are you okay? Ms. Davis?"

"What!"

"Ah!"

The nurse jumps out her skin, turns around to run and smacks her head on the closed door.

"Wait! Nurse I'm sorry! I'm just a little upset about some of the things that happened last night. I didn't mean to snap at you. Please forgive me"

"Well Ms. Davis, You are pretty scary when you're angry. I've got to admit that I have never seen anything like it. I feel sorry for who ever got you that mad."

"I don't know what's happening to me"

"its okay Ms. Davis. The doctor has been checking your blood work since last night. He will be in tonight to talk to you, you'll be fine."

"Thank you Ms. Kathy. Can I call you Ms. Kathy?"

"Sure. In fact you can just call me Kathy. You didn't even touch your food. Just let me know whenever you get finished."

"I'm hungry but I can't eat. You might as well take the tray because I can't eat right now."

"You poor thing, okay but you let me know if you get your appetite back, and I'll get you something to eat."

"Thank you so much, I most definitely will."

When the nurse leaves, Anna turns over and silently cries herself to sleep.

It isn't until 9:00 that night when the doctor shows up. Anna had woken up, watched TV and fell back asleep by then. When she awakes she has a needle in her arm and two small bags of blood over her head going into her veins. Then a man wearing a white coat and a stethoscope walks in the room. In one hand he has a chart and papers, in the other a cup of coffee. He looked like he was in his early 40s. The touch of grey hair gives his age away, otherwise he was in shape and handsome enough to steal action from people half his age. He had a distinguished look about himself in a charismatic sort of way. Anna was surprised to find herself impressed by his good looks and charming appearance.

"How are you doing Ms. Davis? My name is Aaron Page, and I am your doctor this evening. I have checked out your injuries and you are going to be fine."

"I don't have anything to worry about do I?"

"You will be fine"

"Are you sure?"

"Yes I'm sure. You were only bitten right? He didn't try to force himself on you or anything like that?

"No he didn't. But he bit the crap out of me."

"Then you don't have anything, you're not going to get anything from a bit. The nurse told me about your concerns and your symptoms. You'll be okay; you just need some blood so you can get your strength back. You feel a lot better now?"

"I do Doctor Page thank you."

"Okay well there is no sense in keeping you here. I'm going release you so that you can go home."

"Thank you doctor, I was so worried for nothing."

"It's okay. Now you have to remember to be careful out

there and don't forget to eat, that's important too."

"I won't doctor, and I will surely be more careful thank you."

She gets dressed and checks out of the hospital around 10:00 that night. Then calls a taxi and goes straight home. She calls her parents as soon as she gets in the door so they won't worry about her. They try to talk her into coming to stay with them for the night, but she explains that she's safe but tired and has absolutely no plans on going anywhere until tomorrow morning.

Her second call is to her colleagues back at the station. They were glad to know that she was alright and could be able to go home so quickly.

After a shower she got in her robe, turned on the television and relaxed on the couch. Then she started to think about last night. What happened? Yeah forget what could have happened. Let's just be more careful next time. Then it hit her, how is it that she has this decent job, good loving parents, a nice car and her own apartment, and no man, boyfriend or husband. Well maybe she's a little too wild for a husband, not to mention independent. It would still be nice to have someone to come home to who would rub your feet, kiss you from your neck to your lower back, touch you and make sweet love to you. If he could cook afterwards it would blow her freaking mind.

Then the prefect commercial came on at the prefect time. Live links, you know the dating service.

After listening to the commercial she had wrote the number down before it went off and call the number. Anna followed the instructions and placed her greeting.

"Hi guys my name is Anna calling out of Manhattan New York. I'm 23 years of age, 5 foot 6 inches and have long black hair, with brown eyes. I have a nice figure, curves breast and butt, your lucky day. I like movies, bowling, skating, and nice long walks on the beach, but it could be the park. I work as a police officer.

I'm just looking for a genuine good guy. No players please. I'm looking for a long term relationship with a nice honest guy. You don't have to be afraid to tell me if you work at Burger King, a job is a job. I'm not after your money I make plenty, I'm a police officer. Oh shit! I mean!

Then she re-recorded her greeting, this time being very careful to leave out the fact that she was a cop. How in the world are you going to get some if you scare them all away? When she finished her greeting she listened to the guys. The one she liked was calling from out of Rochester NY. His name was Chris. He described himself as being 22 years of age, 5 foot 10, brown hair with brown eyes, medium build and works at Radio Shack. He like skate boarding, football, movies and just hanging out on his spare time. Chris was looking for a nice girl, attractive with a good head on her shoulders. Nice body is definitely a plus. He was looking for a good girl that he would like to adore as even a friend or more.

She beeped in and he answered.

"Hello, how are you?"

"Hi Chris, my name is Anna and I'm feeling you."

"Hi. Can I get your number so I can call you from my cell?"

"You're moving pretty fast."

"No, it's just that this service only gives me a couple of minutes to talk. Them they would charge me an arm and a leg."

"My goodness! Really? No we wouldn't want that to happen, that would suck."

"Yeah it would, but just for my pockets, and phone bill."

"Ok, here it is you got a pen and paper?"

He called her house phone and they got to know each other a little bit more. She learned that he had a younger brother named Tommy who is 13 and is going to start high school next year. Tommy lives with his parents, and Chris right along with them. His best friend is his nerdy co-worker who trained him. The guy's name was David and although he was a computer geek, that didn't stop him from being down for whatever and hanging out anywhere at any time after work. Chris learned that Anna was every bit as sweet as she said she was over the phone. They talked until it was getting late and agreed to speak again later. Anna got in the bed and went straight to sleep for the night.

Came morning around 10am Anna woke up, washed her face and brushed her teeth, got dressed and decided to go to subways and grab a steak sandwich. So she put on her coat and walked out the door. It was very hot out today as she walked back in and took off her coat before going back out again, but this time she put on some shorts and a T-shirt, and some sunscreen lotion then stepped back out hoping that it was good enough this time. Yes it is, much better. She walked down the block to subways and walked in. The line was short so it wasn't a long wait. When she was up she made her order.

"Hi John, how are you doing today?"

"I'm doing good Ms. Davis how are you? Um, Ms. Davis?"

"Yes?"

"Where is your car?"

"The police car?"

"No your car?"

"Oh it's in front of my place. I felt like walking today."

"Aren't you cold?"

"No not really, not at all."

"Ok, what would you like?"

"Can I get a steak sub on wheat bread with steak sauce, along with broccoli and salt & pepper."

"Ok that will be five dollars and forty cents."

She paid him then walked out of the door, before deciding to go see her Mom and Dad. That really would be a nice surprise, plus it's only another 3 blocks away and around the corner.

The sun was hot and bright, why are people walking past her wearing coats and some with hats and scruff. Don't these people know it's hot outside? Well, she would say "whatever" but a lot of weird things and changes have been happening to her every since that man bit her that night. Could it be?

Could it be possible that? No. It's no such thing. So she shook her head and tuned out the idea while at the same time ignoring the funny looks that many people gave her as she continued to walk to her parents place.

She finally reaches her parents building, and her mother buzz her in. "Anna dear what a pleasant surprise," Ms. Carrie said as Anna came up the stairs. Her mother looked at her, then hugged her, then looked at her again. "Anna where is your coat? It's in the car right?"

"No Mom I left the car at home. I felted like walking."

"How come you don't have a coat? And why are you dressed like it's the middle of July?"

"Because it's hot outside Mom."

"Hot outside? It's the middle of October. The leaves are on the ground and it's cold. I mean snow could come down tomorrow."

"Mom give me a break. I just got out of the hospital, and weird things have been happing to me ever since"

"You're right, I'm sorry dear. I'm just glad that you're all right, and you're lucky you didn't have to hear it from your father."

"Where is Dad by the way?"

"He's at the store playing his numbers, but he should be back any minute now"

Ten minutes later her Dad came in.

"Pumpkin you made it."

"Hi Daddy."

"Yeah it's pretty cold out there isn't it? I just bought a couple of new jeans and hood sweaters. You can have a set. You can have one of your mother's scruffs if you like."

"Oh, thank you Daddy."

"Sure thing Pumpkin. You might look like a ninja on the way back home but at least this time you'll be warm."

"Donald honey, she said she was hot."

"Hot? Hot? I had just came back from the store and let me tell you, it could snow tomorrow."

"Yeah Daddy you're right. I think I will take you up on the offer for that ninja suit."

"Ha ha, no problem princess I thought so."

Cold, yeah right. It's hot like a heat wave outside. Good thing she didn't mention to them about the sunscreen lotion or they might admit her to the mental ward. She gave her Mom and Dad the steak sub to split, and told them that she ate one so that they wouldn't feel bad or try to pressure her to eat something. The truth was that she ate nothing, all day and all that afternoon and tried with success to ignore her hunger, and enjoy spending time with her parents, before she finally left for home between 8:30 and 8:45.

When Anna reaches her home, there is a Black SUV parked in front of her place. Ok this is unusual, this truck doesn't look familiar at all. Its back windows are heavily tinted, and the front lightly so. That part is normal for any SUV. Anna looks once. Wait a minute, she looks again and notices a person still sitting in the driver side of the car. Man this guy or girl whoever it is looks like he or she is stalking somebody if you let her tell it. Or perhaps it's an undercover cop, who knows. She gives the person one of those looks that says "I may not know who you are, but I got my eye on you" then heads for her building.

"Hey! Hello Ms. Davis is that you?"

Well it's definitely a man. Anna is kind of startled. She's also wearing those black jeans and hood sweater, along with a black scarf tied around her face and the hood over her head, just like a ninja. It was pretty impressive that he still recognized her. Even more importantly, why does he know her when she doesn't know him? She thinks to herself that she should just clam down and see what he wanted. She takes her hood down and scarf off, then turns around.

"Ms. Davis is that you?"

"Yes it is. Hello and who are you?"

Wait a minute; she knows exactly who he is. The man from the hospital, It's her doctor. What would bring him to her place? Especially unannounced? It's either that, or he randomly wandered in front of her place.

"It's me, Doctor Page from the hospital. I just figured that I would stop by and check to see how you were doing."

"It's just you. Well why didn't you just call Doctor?"

"Oh I did 10 minutes ago and left a message, but since I was in the neighborhood I figured I would see if you were home yet so that maybe I get a chance to talk to you one on one about some of my concerns."

"Concerns? You told me that I was ok, now you're saying that something might be wrong with me?"

"May I have a word with you?"

"Sure, what is it?"

"May I come in so we can talk in private?"

"What?"

"Privacy protection Ms. Davis."

"I'm going to get an order of protection Dr. Page."

"I see. Okay then have a good night."

"I'm just kidding doctor, come in."

The doctor grabs a clipboard and briefcase and follows her inside the apartment.

"So what's wrong with me Doctor Page?"

"Well do you remember the night that you got bit?"

"Yes I remember it well."

"You have been feeling a little strange ever since?"

"Very indeed, go on."

"Do you still have that scar on your neck?"

"I don't know let me check, of course I would."

She goes to the bathroom, turns on the light and looks into the mirror. That's strange, she can't find the scar. She pulls her left and right shirt collar down. Nothing. That doesn't make sense. Bewildered, she walks back to the living room and took a seat on the couch next to her doctor.

"Ms. Davis? Ms. Davis?"

"Oh huh?"

"It's ok, I have something that will help."

"Ok."

He opens up his briefcase and takes out a needle connected to a tube.

"Medicine?"

"Yes. I would like you to try this. You will feel a thousand percent better. May I?"

"Yeah I'm ready. Go ahead."

He attaches the needle and tube to something inside his briefcase and then puts the needle in her arm.

"So Ms. Davis, how have you been holding up so far? Are you still eating?"

"No, now that you mention it I haven't eaten anything since."

"Don't worry about it. Your mom and Dad came to see you first thing that morning. The nurse told me. She also says that you're a real feisty woman and a real head cracker."

She couldn't help herself, she had to laugh. It's was nice that he could make her laugh. "You mean firecracker?"

"Yes. How have things been with your job?"

"Ok I guess. I let them know that I was back home last night, and they are giving me a couple of days off."

"Did you go outside at all today?"

"Yeah it was hot, I had to wear suntan lotion. Please don't call me crazy. Besides, you just saw me come in."

"Well yeah you're right, and no dear you're not crazy. The sun is hot. From now on you should try staying out of the sun."

"What?"

"Oh, and keep this between me and you. We don't want to scare anybody."

Did he just say we don't want to scare anybody? That was it. Anna glances down at the needle in her arm and notices a red liquid flowing from whatever was in the briefcase, though the tube and into her arm. She was starting to feel better until her eyes betrayed her. This looks too freaky for her.

"Doctor Page?"

"Yes dear."

"What is this stuff going into my arm?"

"Do you feel better my dear?"

"Yes."

"Good. Now I have to get going, I'm running late for work."

He removes the needle and tube from her arm and puts it back into the briefcase, then puts on his coat before heading to the door.

"Wait, Doctor Page."

"Oh I'm sorry, here is my cell and house number. Call me if you need me anytime, except for tonight. You're young and beautiful. I wouldn't let life pass me by. Think about it and let me know. Oh look at the time."

He rushes out of the door while looking at his watch. Anna just stands there until she hears the start of his engine. Then she ran out the door in an attempt to catch up with him. By the time she ran down the porch stairs, he was already down the street. Maybe she can still get his attention. She started to run down the sidewalk.

"Doctor. Page! Doctor Page wait!"

He didn't see or hear her. By the time she took her 8th step, he had already turned the corner.

"Hey! Shit! Shit! Shit! This is bullshit!"

The time is 10:00pm and Anna looks like a real crazy lady right now. A man she knew yelled out of the window of his apartment.

"Sister Davis are you alright?"

"I'm okay Robert. I'm just having a bad day. Sorry."

"It's alright Ms. Davis. If there is anything I can do for you let me know anytime."

"Thank you but I'm ok. Just one of those days that seem like bad luck that's all."

2

Back inside the house, Anna locks the door and sits in a chair. The phone rings.

"How are you doing babygirl?"

"Hi Chris. Look, I'm having a real bad night, so if at any point

I sound like the wicked witch of the west, please understand."

"It's okay. If you're having a bad day and you need someone to talk to, I will be here."

"Thank you. That's what half of the problem has been lately. No one to talk to when life as you know it turns upside down." Anna took a breath. "I got attacked a couple nights ago."

"Ah man, you call the police?"

"Damn-it I am a… friend of a police officer."

"Okay okay, just calm down and don't kill me."

"I'm sorry Chris. I'm not mad at you."

"Yeah you sound like you been though a lot lately. Who's your police friend?"

"My best friend's name is Kyle Miller. He's a Detective I've known for years."

"My advice would be to call him up if he's available, and go out somewhere for a couple of hours. Then when you come back invite a friend to stay the night with you."

"That's not a bad idea."

"Yeah but keep in mind that I like you. Not trying to tell you what to do or anything but..."

"I know, you don't have to worry, I'm only kicking it with you. In fact, I think I'll call my girlfriend over too. She would love to hang out."

"All three of you are going out? That's what I'm talking about. Just make sure you call me back to let me know they showed up and you're safe ok?"

"I will let you know soon as they show."

"Cool, spend the night out girl. Call them now."

Brenda is a rather wild friend of hers. There were times when Anna had to throw her in the back of the police car herself. Luckily for Brenda, Anna was a friend of hers from a long time ago and kept releasing her to her grandmother in Queens.

"Hello Brenda? This is Anna. What are you doing right now?"

"Nothing, why what's up?"

"You want to hang with me? I'm bored."

"Oh I can't right now girl I'm kind of... you know."

"High? So what? Bring me a bag of weed too. Just bring your light skinned butt over."

"You for real? So you're a free spirit tonight huh? Well I don't know."

"I've got full cable, a Playstation 3, and almost every game for it in the store."

Then Brenda's little brother overheard the conversation.

"Brenda can I come too?"

"No Brandon its girl's night out. Mom won't let you go anywhere this time of night anyway. Its 10:30."

"She let you go."

"I'm nineteen."

"That's your little Brother?"

"Yeah, our Mom is so protective of him I'm almost jealous. Almost. Hey Brandon, when I come back I promise I will bring you back an ice cream."

While Anna waits on Brenda, she calls Kyle Miller to ask him if he would take her and her girlfriend out somewhere. Maybe to dinner at the sports bar.

"You want me to pay for you and your friend?"

"No silly, my treat okay? Will you pick us up?"

"Yeah give me 15 minutes. Oh, and you don't have to pay my way. I'm treating you."

"No I'm treating you, this time."

"Okay, this time. I'm on the way."

Seven minutes later, Brenda rings the doorbell.

"Hey girl."

"Hi. Glad you could make it. My friend Kyle is coming in a minute to pick us up and take us out."

"I'm not dressed to go out. Besides, who is Kyle? Another police officer?"

"Yes he's a detective."

"No way, I don't know him. That's your friend."

"I'm sorry, I should have checked with you."

"It's cool. I will be free tomorrow."

When Kyle comes in, both girls notice that he was the only one dressed to go out. He is in everything but the suit: nice tan slacks and blazer to match. Anna still has on her black jeans but she put on a brown Baby Phat t-shirt. Brenda on the other hand, is wearing pink sweat pants with a red hood shirt, too perfectly mismatched.

"Hey why don't y'all two go out? I'm not prepared."

"Would you like us to drop you off home? Miss?"

"Greenmen, Brenda Greenmen. Actually I was going to stay here for a while until Anna gets back."

Anna nods. "You just want to check out some channels and play that game don't you? You're welcome to anything in that fridge or freezer, but I don't have anything already cooked."

"I've got shrimp in the freezer."

"Don't eat it all. Save me at least half."

"I just want a couple, but I'd settle for baloney and cheese. Thank you Anna."

"Hey, I'll be back in two hours."

Five minutes later the phone rings. Brenda is about to start boiling the water for the shrimp when she hears three loud clicks from the other room, followed by Anna's voice broadcasting her outgoing message. She smiles as she leans against the kitchen doorway. No cell phone and she actually has an answering machine.

"Hey Anna dear, it's your Mother. If you're home please pick up. Two girls came by looking for you a minute ago. A girl named Carol and your other friend Donna, or something. They were kind of on the pushy side. They told me that it was very important that they get in contact with you. They wanted to know where to find you. When I told them to give me their numbers so you could call them, they wanted me to buzz them up so they could talk to me in person. I told Carol to hold on so I could call you first, and they told me not to worry about that and they are supposed to come back tomorrow afternoon. Is everything okay? Call me as soon as you get this. Bye."

Brenda stops smiling, looks at the phone and scratches her head. Did something happen? Anna and Kyle just left five minutes ago. Did something happen earlier that day? Let's find out when Anna gets back, she thinks. Anna is more likely to talk to Kyle about whatever it was. Right now they are out trying to have a good time. Then she thinks about her mother and her little brother Brandon. What if she was worrying her mother all this time while being out at all those wild parties? What if Brandon grows up a sucker for all the wrong women or in and out of jail because she never spent any time with him? No way will she let this happen. Brenda makes a genuine pledge to herself to spend more time with her family and do more around the house. For now, she will hook up the Playstation and play a couple of games until Anna returns.

Meanwhile, a few blocks away, Carol and Donna have just left Anna's parents' building. "That's real messed up Carol. She didn't even buzz us in."

"Yeah usually older people are a little more cautious. You know, she's probably the don't-talk-to-strangers type."

"She's probably at the hospital. James wants to give her a chance to join us. I wish I could kill her. That bitch shot me four times and I want to return the favor."

"I bet you do. That's why I sent James to the hospital, and you're with me. She's too dangerous for us, and I don't like her ether. Oh, and she's not at the hospital. I called."

"What if James gets mad?"

"Donna?"

"Yes?" Carol didn't answer.

"I know, I know, you're older than James."

"By almost fifty damn years. Plus he doesn't have to know. I don't want to have to pull rank all the time."

A teenage boy runs up and snatches Donna's purse. Carol quickly grabs him and pulls him back. Donna grabs him by the neck and yells at him.

"Boy, I am not in the mood this!" Carol is laughing. Donna is choking the crap out of this teenager. When she realizes this, she turns his neck loose and grabs his shirt collar. He punches her in the mouth and tries to run again. Donna yanks him again by the back of his shirt. "Where do you think you're going so fast you little brat?!"

"Ahh! Bitch get off me!"

"What did you call me?"

The kid pulls out a .22 caliber and points it at her face. This makes Donna incredibly angry. She puts her hand over the hammer and rips the gun from his hand. Then she grabs him again by the neck with her other hand, she picks him up and violently shook him.

"You brat! Don't you know I've had it up to here with guns in my face! Huh!"

"Let go. Plea..."

"Why, because you're stupid? Do you want to go home? Huh? Huh? Huh!"

The neck snaps.

"Oops, ah, um."

"Well Donna" Carol laughs. "That wasn't very nice."

"But I wasn't trying to kill him. I was just trying to scare him."

"Well he looks pretty scared to me. He's not dead yet. See kid? You could have been somebody."

"Somebody help me. Ma, momma, ma..."

"Oh no. Come on Donna lets go, and give me the gun."

Carol takes the gun from Donna and gets five or six steps before she realizes that Donna isn't beside or behind her. So she turns around and, Donna is biting him.

"Oh come on. You can eat later; we don't have time for this right now."

Carol folds her arms and turns her head in irritation as she waits for her clumsy grand pupil to hurry up with her meal. When she turns and looks again, what she sees kind of shocks her.

"Yo Donna, what the hell are you doing?"

Donna has her wrist cut and against his mouth. The boy is trying to spit the blood back out and Donna is getting frustrated with him. So she whispers softly.

"It's okay stupid brat, drink. It's good for you."

"I see that you've lost your mind, but you can't change him or anyone else without the permission of the council."

"But I feel so bad for him."

"First of all, you are bad. Second, give him to me."

"What?"

"I'm trained. I can help."

Carol goes to him and snaps his neck all the way, killing him instantly.

"No!"

"He didn't feel a thing. Now let's go."

They walk away. Carol takes the gun from Donna and shoots a witness, and then another, and at another, until the street clears of people. *They run though the alley cut and get out of the area.* They beat up a couple and took their clothes. Donna punches the girl and breaks her jaw. Carol throws the guy against a brick wall and punches him in the mouth, knocking him out cold. Once they've changed clothes, Carol gives Donna a small lecture about the ropes.

"You know I got to tell you, you are becoming one of those stupid new Buddhist-acting vampires with their 'let's not kill anybody and live together' bullshit."

"No I'm not. Carol those pint bags don't taste that good. It's cold and kind of nasty. Kind of like when we use to eat spinach in a can or spam - a poor man's meal. You remember eating that dog food? You know, back when we were human?

"Hmm... let me think. Nope, can't say that I do. Well at least right now. Look, the point is we don't change people without the permission of the council. We don't let people know we exist, and most importantly, we kill people who find out."

"But what about the elders? They eat pint bags a lot of the times, and people know about them. Why we have to live like fugitives? Even when Halloween is coming up in two weeks?"

"Hey. First of all, the elders only eat pints when the police start to pay attention to the body count, or missing people who are important. Second, the only people who know about them are people they trust. Powerful people and organizations they have known and trusted for I don't even know how long."

"When am I going to get a chance to meet an elder?"

"Well I'm 90, and was turned at 27 by a lady named Stephanie. Stephanie Page. She's like 200 years old. 165 years ago her husband had turned her after she had caught scarlet fever back in Ireland. He warned his girl at the time that he was bitten last month and that he was a vampire, and that she would die without his help. At first she said no, but two days later she said yes. He bit her and cut his wrist so that she could drink. Then he took her and they fled Ireland to come here and he married her."

"Wow, can they actually tell me about the civil war?"

"Look, just whenever you get to meet her just be respectful, and keep your mouth shut about our little conversation."

"What did you used to do? You know, before she turned you?"

"I was a carhop at an A & W Restaurant. I was coming home from work one night when I was attacked. She was going to kill me, but I cried and used the 'I got to get home to my kids' lie. Then for some reason she let me live. She doesn't let anyone live, It's the rule. Forty-seven years later I met this one cute guy."

"James?"

"Yes. He was 24 at the time, he asked me out one night and I said yes. He took me out to the movies at the drive-in. Once we were in the back seat of his car, while he was inside me I bit him. He said 'what are you doing?' I stopped and realized something. I love that man, and he loved me, until he found out that I was a real vampire. He was ridiculously mad at me for months."

"Oh I love to bite, that's got to be better than sex. I'm jealous."

Carol raises her hand and almost slaps her. Donna jumps and covers her face. "Carol chill!"

"I'm sorry Donna I usually don't snap like that."

"I thought so. Don't let me have to kick your ass."

Carol just looks at her. Donna gives her a playful smile, and Carol puts her arm around Donna's shoulder. They walk past a Subway store. Carol and Donna overhear the cashier talking to a customer about what happened to Ms. Davis three nights ago. Yes that's got to be her. Carol and Donna walk into the store right past the customer who was leaving, and for a moment, it's just Donna, Carol, and the casher. The time is 11:38. Carol does the talking.

"Hi, my name is Wendy. What can I do for you Ladies?"

"Hello, I noticed you were talking about Ms. Davis. We are her friends."

"Really? That's cool, *what's your name*?"

"You know I got to check on my girl, and I brought my little body guard with me."

"Ha ha ha! The three of us only weigh a buck and some change, but that's smart thinking. Not walking out here at night alone. *What are your names?*"

"Oh were from Long Island. We came as soon as we heard what happened. She's going to be so mad at us for not coming sooner."

"No she won't, I wouldn't be. You guys just found out tonight?"

"Yeah! My friend was already dressed. I threw on my daddy's coat and got moving."

"I wish that I had friends like that."

"We are not that familiar with this area, especially at night."

"Really? Well Anna lives right down the street. You're almost there, Just a half a block farther right. There at that brown and yellow building. Come outside for a second and I will show you."

The casher takes them outside and points at the building down the street.

"See that brown and yellow building over there? I think its 325 or 327, but it's that building right there."

"Thank you Wendy. Which floor?"

"I believe it's downstairs. The first floor, Come on, you're supposed to at least remember that much."

"Yeah that's true. I'm sorry; I'm just like a chicken with my head cut off right now. I'm moving faster than I can think right now."

"Girl I know what you mean, but she will be so happy to see you guys."

"Thank you. We have got to get going."

"Hey wait."

"Yes."

"Take care of her for me okay."

Carol and Donna both look at each other with an evil smile. They burst out laughing like Betty and Wilma, and answer together:

"We will!"

At the sports bar, Anna and Kyle are having a good time while watching the UFC pay-per-view event on the giant screen TV. Kyle has ordered Chinese egg fried rice and shrimp, with a pitcher of Bud to drink.

"Oh go ahead. You know you can get whatever you like.

Help me drink this beer, anyway."

"Thank you but I will just order a little later."

"Ok, no rush."

"Kyle I'm so glad that you could make it."

"That's what friends are for."

"You're the best."

"Yeah I'm just waiting on my ex-wife to figure that out."

"Jeanne? Forget about her, she was stupid anyway. She's

probably kicking herself right now."

"Probably, but it was only three months ago."

"Yeah well how long have you known her?"

"Only two years but still. Her whole thing was that I didn't

have enough time for her."

"Ok I'm going to be honest, so don't get mad at me ok?"

"Oh no, alright go ahead and shoot my heart out."

"No it's nothing against you; it's about your ex-wife. She was

a stupid, gold-digging bimbo anyway. I mean she was a

waitress at the waffle house. That was cool until she quit her job two weeks after marrying you. Hell, I should have listened to my intuition when you introduced her to me the first time.

She kept looking at me like she won the lottery. I should have pulled you to the side and said something."

"You did, you said, 'I don't like that alley cat.' And you said that I should get rid of her very quickly."

"Yeah I did, didn't I?"

"But I didn't listen. I said give her a chance."

"You said, 'but she's a nice girl, and she's going to be Mrs. Miller in four months.' and she divorced you a year and a half later and tried to sue you for alimony and maintenance. She even pissed me off."

"Well I'm glad you stayed of out it. I didn't even want you to be in that one."

"Ha. Do you remember your first court date?"

"Yeah she never made it. That was funny. She said that some young light skinned girl robbed her."

"Ha! And what about the second time she tried to come?"

"Oh I remember that one well." Kyle laughs. "The Judge had

rescheduled Jeanne to come back, her tire was flat. She called a cab, and then the cab driver got a ticket. Running a red light."

"Clemens fixed the ticket and let him go. He didn't run a light. We offered him a better job for his troubles. Today he works for a car service downtown."

"That was you?"

"Let's just say that I got your back. She tried a third time. I called her and told her that her court date was rescheduled until the next week."

"But she also got a letter."

"Yeah I know, in disappearing ink."

"I thought she was lying when she said she got that letter, then the pages turned blank."

"Didn't everybody?"

"Anna?"

"Yes."

"You are an angel. What would I have ever done without you?"

"Oh, you would have been taking it up the rear. What are

friends for? Now I think I deserve a glass of that beer."

She pours herself a glass of beer from the pitcher and drinks and nothing happens. She asks Kyle for some of his food. As soon as she tastes it, she knows that she can't swallow it, but at least she can look at it without her stomach flipping, and put food in her mouth without an allergic reaction. So she tries to chew and swallow, but once again starts retching.

"Anna are you ok?"

"Yeah it must've gone down the wrong pipe."

Anna is grateful that it wasn't half as bad as the last time she tried to eat. Whatever the Doctor gave her is definitely helping her with that stomach virus or throat cold or whatever it is. She remembers somebody telling her that life is short. She excuses herself to go to the ladies' room, and on the way back stops at the end of the bar and settles the bill.

Two men sitting across the room look at Kyle and Anna for a moment, then get up and start walking over. One is a fairly short stocky guy with Black hair and a thin mustache and beard. He is wearing blue jeans and a black T-shirt with a matching black ball cap, and has to be in his mid-30s. The other guy looks a little like Kyle: medium build, brown hair, clean-shaven and in his early 40s in blue jeans and a green jersey. The taller of the two speaks first.

"Hey Kyle, we thought that was you. How you been?"

"Hey long time no see. Anna this is John."

"Hi."

"And the short guy over here is Stanley."

"You look great."

"Thank you."

Stanley wants to ask him if she's his girlfriend, but waits for one of them to come out and claim the other. So far it's not happening.

"So Kyle, Anna, what brings you two guys out here tonight?"

"We just decided to chill out take it easy for a night and have a good time."

"Sounds like somebody was getting in trouble."

Anna speaks up. "He's not in any trouble at all."

"What? Well Mr. Miller you are one lucky man."

"I wish? Anna and I are only friends."

"See baby I was trying to… now why did you have to go and say a thing like that?"

"Uh-oh. Now you're in trouble. Don't kill him sugar he's a good guy."

"I know." Anna changes the subject. "Say, what do you guys do for a living?"

They don't seem to want to answer that question, but Stanley says,

"We're bounty hunters."

"Okay, that's a good job. Why are you guys ashamed to tell me?"

"Because we're looking for a guy right now, he ran out on his bail."

"I understand. I'm a police officer myself. Your secret is safe with me."

"Kyle you didn't tell us she was police."

"Yeah. She joined the force three years ago. She is as smart, strong and brave as she is beautiful. She's my angel."

"Oooh, Kyle thank you."

"Kyle you better hold on to her, or you're going to be kicking yourself for three years."

Anna starts blushing, and John gives Kyle a "that's' a keeper" look and Stanley smiles, shrugs a little and looks at his watch. "Time flew. Sorry but it's 12:35 and we had better get going."

"Oh, yeah it's time. Good thing that one of us was paying attention."

"Let me get your numbers so that we don't lose contact again."

"Kyle I have to get home too. I have to be considerate to Brenda."

"You should call her."

"That's a good idea."

She calls the apartment from Kyle's phone, but no one answers and the machine picks up.

"No answer?"

"Nope. Maybe she's asleep. I better start heading back."

"Okay. That was a quick two hours huh?"

"I know right?"

They leave out of the sports bar in Kyle's Escalade. As they pull off, Kyle notices that he's a little popped from those beers. Not badly, just a little.

"Kyle are you ok?"

"Yeah just a little buzzed, that's all."

"Do you want me to drive?"

"That might be a good idea. Here, let me pull over at this gas station and top off the tank. We can switch seats there."

He pulls into the Sunoco station, gets out, and walks into the store. Anna gets out and tries to pump the gas but the gas cap has a lock on it, so she gets back in the truck and in the driver's seat and adjusts the mirrors. Moving the rearview down so she could see herself, Anna screams. She quickly put her hand over her mouth and screams again. She looks at the other mirrors on the truck, and nothing, nothing except the back of the truck and the lot behind it. She sits frozen, with her hands on the wheel.

Kyle has come back, after pumping his gas, and got in the passenger side. When he looks at her, she breaks her gaze and looks back at him.

"Anna? Are you ok?"

She only gives him a blank stare.

"Anna!"

"Huh? Yeah?"

"You look like you've just seen a ghost. What's going on?"

"Nothing, It's just been a long day."

"You're keeping something from me. Why? Are you ok? You know you're not alone."

"I've just looked in the… I will tell you when we get to the house I promise, but for now you should drive."

So Kyle takes the wheel, and they drive back to her place. As they round the corner of her street, they notice fire trucks and police cars. Kyle worries that it might be Anna's place, and she worries right along with him. Neither can tell what apartment it was until they got a little closer.

It is Anna's apartment. They both watch in horror as they drive up as close as the on-duty police officers would allow them. Kyle parks the truck, and they get out and walk up to the building. Before they reach the first step, two detectives stop them.

"Excuse me Sir, Ma'am, do you live here?"

"I do. My name is Anna Davis. I'm a police officer." *She reaches in her pocket and pulls out her badge.*

"Ok Officer Davis, you don't mind if we ask you a couple of questions?"

"Well first of all, my name is Detective Robison, and this is my partner Sharon Walker."

"How do you do Officer Davis?"

"Fine, how are you?"

Detective Robison get a kick out of it.

"Ha ha ha, Ah man. Okay sorry about that ladies, that greeting was kind of a classic. You're a police officer?"

"Yes, yes I am."

Sharon takes over.

"Excuse me, but do you know who was in your house tonight?"

"Yes I do. My friend Brenda Greenmen was the only one here while I was gone. No one else."

"Do you know anybody who would want to harm you for any reason?"

"No not really. I mean, I have a couple of run-ins and bad nights every once in a while, but I don't have any enemies."

Kyle intervenes with a question of his own. Not rudely but assertively.

"Excuse me for just a second. Kyle Miller, Major Cases. Would you mind telling me what happened? And what kind of evidence do you have here?" Both, Robison and Sharon look at each other. They know that name sounds familiar,

"Officer Anna Davis is a friend of mine" said Kyle. But this is not a social gathering.

Detective Robison explains to Anna and Kyle what had happened to the best of his knowledge. "Well, it's been kind of a crazy night so bear with me. Your neighbor called in and reporting gunshots. When we arrived at the scene, it looked like somebody did indeed shoot up your place Officer Davis. We found a couple of dints on the hood of this 2008 Dodge

Impala parked in front of your place."

"That's my Car!"

"It appears that whoever did this stood on your car, and used it as leverage to shoot in though your window. The curtain was closed and there was a person inside sitting right here on this chair watching TV.

"My friend Brenda."

"So your friend Brenda was sitting right here, when the first bullet came through the front window and through the curtain, then hit the wall near her. She had to duck by the second and third shot because two more shots were fired, and killed your chair."

Then Detective Robison motions everyone to follow.

"Now you see this right here?"

Kyle and Anna looked at each other.

"I want you guys to climb up here and take a look at this."

Then Detective Robison climbs on the hood of the 2008 Dodge Impala. Kyle and Sharon follow him to the top the car. Anna starts pulling her hair, but it goes unnoticed as the detectives talk. Robison explains. "All right check this out.

Take a look through this window here."

"I'm looking Robison. The light is on but I don't see anything."

"Well the only thing I see is a curtain and some shadows of some things in the house, and a couple of small bullet holes. That's about it."

"Exactly! See, whoever did this couldn't clearly see who they were shooting at."

"So they thought they were shooting at Anna?"

"That's right Kyle, and what do you think Sharon?"

"I think you're on a roll Mr. Robison. We might crack this case tonight."

Then Anna had interrupted them with a few words of her own.

"I think all three of you are on to something, my car! The three of you are going to crack my windshield."

"Oh! Sorry Ms. Davis."

"Sorry about that Anna. "

"Officer Davis, I am sorry."

All three detectives climb down off of the hood of her twenty thousand dollar vehicle. Sharon slips and adds another dint on the hood, along with a small scratch while coming down. Anna clenches her teeth. She wants to punch her in the face, although Sharon apologized again. Kyle knows that Anna's still angry, so he takes her aside. "Anna please don't be mad at her or us for that matter. They don't mean to be rude or anything. But what about your friend Brenda?"

"I'm sorry Kyle your right. Wait a minute, you know I'm not mad at you, and I can't be upset with Robison.

Then she looks back.

"And Detective Sharon?"

"Yes Anna?"

"Its okay don't worry about it. You guys are doing an excellent job."

Then Detective Robison finishes explaining what happened, according to his evidence.

"Now, Brenda had dodged getting shot. We found the back door open, and there were signs of a scuffle in the back yard. She must have run out the back door to try to escape the situation. That's all we have for now, we don't know what else happened yet."

"Well detectives, do you mind if I go and take a look around for myself?"

"Sure Ms. Davis, but don't contaminate anything. CSU is still in there. Detective Miller, can you accompany Officer Davis inside? I don't think there's any more evidence to find, but you know how they are. We think that whoever the attackers were, they never entered the apartment. There's no blood or body in the back, so we don't think this is a murder case. I'm afraid they'll be in there for a while."

Kyle says. "She's staying with me tonight. Anna needs to get some sleep. If you need her, you can reach me at home."

Anna and Kyle walk in and look around. It looks just like Robison described, with no sign of Brenda anywhere, or anyone else.

"So I'm staying with you tonight?"

"Let's just say that I got your back."

3

Anna puts a change of clothes in a bag, then turns off the lights and follows him out the door. They take Kyle's ride and drive to his apartment. When they get to the door of Kyle's apartment, Anna tries to follow him in. "Ouch! Ouch!"

"Ouch? What happened?"

"I don't know, I got shocked or something."

She tries again. A shock runs through her body and she is pushed back from the threshold.

"Ouch ouch! I'm getting shocked, and I feel like something is throwing me back."

"What? The door is wide open. Come in, and stop acting like you've lost your mind."

"But I'm going to get… never mind, you'll see watch."

He watches as she tries to enter the apartment. This time nothing happens, and Anna walks in. What the heck was that about? "Okay I'm in."

"My goodness Anna am I going to have to call you a shrink?"

"No, at least I don't think so."

"You know what? That reminds me. You promised me that you would tell me what was going on as soon as we got to your place."

"But we just left my place."

"Yes we did, and now we're at my place and an explanation is overdue."

"Okay fine, but promise me you won't get mad."

"Why would I get mad? I promise you I won't get mad."

"Okay, do you remember that night I got attacked?"

"Yes, it was three nights ago."

"Remember when I told you that I thought the people were vampires and the guy bit me?"

"Yeah, but there are no such thing as vampires"

"Remember when you asked me what I saw in the truck while you were in the store?"

"Yeah, you expect me to believe that you're turning into some sort of vampire?"

"Come in the bathroom with me. I want to show you something."

"Show me what?"

"Oh Kyle, just come in the bathroom. You go in first in, then turn on the light and look in the mirror."

"Fine but I still don't see where you're getting at."

Kyle goes through the doorway to the bathroom, turns to his right and flips on the light. He steps over to the mirror above the sink and calls back to her, "Okay I'm looking in the mirror. What am I supposed to see?"

"Just keep looking." Anna walks in and stands right behind him. She gets up on her toes and looks over his shoulder. Over the other, she waves her hand at the mirror. "Hey Kyle, what do you see?"

"I see that you're hiding behind me."

Anna slips around his right, brushing a bath towel hanging on a bar. Kyle is a little confused, but before he can make sense of what he's seeing, Anna is in front of him, holding his left hand in hers. She reaches over to the bar, takes a hand towel and flips it up on to her head.

"Ahhh!"

Anna knew what she would see, but she was not prepared for how disturbing the image would be. Kyle's scream dissolves the last of her courage. She clutches his hand tight, pressing it against her chest and screams right back at him, kicking off another round of screams.

Ahhhh! You said that you wouldn't get mad!"

"I'm not mad; I'm freaked out!"

"What do I do?"

"I don't know!"

"Well I was trying to tell you."

Kyle composes himself a little. "I need a drink."

"But we had drinks."

"Well then I need to lay down."

Kyle lies down on the bed. Anna sits up next to him. There is no way she's going to sleep tonight. "Kyle?"

"Yes?"

"I knew you was still up. Do you have any meat in the freezer?"

"Yes I have a couple of T-bone steaks, some chicken, and some lamb chops."

"Can I have a T-bone steak?"

"Oh, now you're Hungry? Sure go ahead."

She goes into the kitchen and takes out two T-bone steaks and a three-pack of lamb chops and lets them thaw on the table, looking at the red fluid clinging to the plastic and the solid flesh beneath it. When she lies down again, she rubs Kyle's head until he falls asleep.

Come morning, Kyle is awake and has called in to work. It has been quiet a night. Anna has finally fallen asleep. He goes to the kitchen to fix breakfast. Bacon and eggs with grits, or pancakes and sausage? Before he can make up his mind, he remembers that Anna had taken some meat out to cook last night. His two T-bone steaks are missing, and all three lamb chops. No way did she eat all that, even if she had help. He checks the garbage can. There are the plastic bags, and with his meat still in them. Why would she throw away his meat? At first he figured that she must have left it out and it spoiled overnight. Over 30 dollars worth of food was gone to waste. Well it happens. Maybe they were freezer burned in the first place. He looks though the bags and notices that his once juicy steaks and lamb chops, now looked like someone could have mistaken it for bubble gum. They look like she never even cooked them.

He puts the bag of chewed up food back in the garbage, and washes his hands. He grabs his cigarettes and lighter, but can't keep his hands still. On the third try, he gets one lit and pours himself a scotch. Feeling a little steadier, he puts the smoke in his mouth, and carries the drink and an ashtray from the kitchen table slowly, like a man who is not sure if the floor beneath him actually exists, to the living room couch. He turns the TV on to see the News.

Anna wakes up and comes out of the bedroom.

"Good morning."

"Good morning Anna."

"Oh, the News is on. Can I call my parents and let them know that I'm ok? I want to talk to them before they see the news or find out from someone else." Kyle hands her his phone.

"Hi Dad it's me."

" Hi Pumpkin, I'm glad you called. How have you been?"

"I'm okay daddy, so don't be worried okay?"

"Worried about what? Did something happen again?"

" You didn't see the News yet?"

"No Pumpkin I didn't. Hold on, let me turn on the TV right
now."

"No! Daddy no. I want to talk to you first and let you know
that I'm alright."

"Okay okay, but what happened? Your mother tried to call
you last night. She said somebody came looking for you or
something like that."

"Really? Who?"

"I don't know sweetheart. I wasn't really paying attention.
One of your friends or something. I'll ask your mother when
she gets back, she went over down the street to see her
friend Maria."

"Okay I'll ask Mom whenever she gets back."

" Wait a minute. What happened? What will I see on the News?"

"While I was out, my apartment got shot up."

"Your apartment got shot up?!"

"My girlfriend was at my place, and I was at the sports bar with another friend"

"What? That doesn't make any sense. You left with one friend, left another friend at the apartment, and your apartment got shot up?"

"Yeah, it's a long story. I don't even know what happened. All I know is that when I came back, the police and fire trucks were everywhere. They said that someone shot through my window."

"What about your friend at your apartment? Is she ok?"

"She's missing. We are trying to find out what happened, if she's all right and where she is now. Can I call you back a little later?"

"Sure, but keep me posted okay?"

"Absolutely."

While Anna is in the bathroom to freshening up, there is a knock on the apartment door. She hears Kyle's voice. "Who is it?"

"It's me, Jeanne."

"What's up?"

"Can I talk to you for a minute?"

"Yeah." Kyle lets her in.

"Hey Kyle how have you been?"

"Okay I guess."

"Good, I hope you're not still mad at me. You know I've missed you right?"

"Yeah right. Don't you have a boyfriend?"

"Well yeah but, I came to see you. Why don't we chill together for a while? Just me and you?"

Anna comes out of the bathroom.

"And me."

"Who the hell are you?"

"Hi Jeanne, I'm Anna. Remember me?"

"Kyle what is she doing here?"

"Huh? Jeanne are you serious?"

"You're right Kyle. I can't get mad, so can we talk for a minute?"

Kyle sits down on the couch and fires a look at Anna: "help."

Anna smiles, comes over and sits on Kyle's lap. "Let's talk."

Kyle's chin drops for only a moment. He recovers quickly and plays it smooth. Jeanne on the other hand is furious, her face turned red as a tomato. Anna whispers in Kyle's ear, asks if she could get rid of Jeanne. Kyle nods, then Jeanne speaks to Kyle.

"Well if you have company, I can come back later."

"I don't know why, he will in bed asleep."

"Okay, see you later. Ciao."

" Hey Jeanne."

"Yeah what's up?"

"I will be here later too."

"Bitch you are making my blood boil, get smart with me one more time!"

Anna raises her eyebrows, and jumps off of Kyle's at Jeanne. Kyle tries to pull her back to his lap, but he can't hold her and he nearly falls on the floor. He just manages to hold on to her with both arms as she keeps right on going toward Jeanne. She drags him five feet before she even notices him holding her. One thing was for sure, he can not stop this tiny woman.

"Anna wait."

"What why? Sure okay." Jeanne is off running out the door, down the hall and down the stairs. "Yeah you better run!" Anna turns to Kyle and surprises him. "Hey, you want to finish what we started?"

"What do you mean?"

"You know."

He smacks her booty, she smiles, and he puts one arm around her waist to pull her close. He kisses her and she kisses him back. He picks her up and lays her on the couch. He is kissing her again, then the phone rings. He checks to see who's calling before he turning off the ringer, but the caller ID says Mr. and Mrs. Davis. "It's your dad calling back."

"Can I get it Kyle?"

"Sure go ahead."

"Hello Anna? Is that you?"

"Yes it's me. Hi, Mom."

"I just got in the door and you father told me your house got shot up, are you okay? Oh yeah, there were two girls who came by looking for you last night."

"Who were they?"

"If I remember correctly, it was Carol and Donna. They wanted to talk to you and they said it was important. I left a message on your answering machine as soon as they left."

"Thank you. I will go back to the house and check it out."

"Where are you now? Whose number is this?"

"I'm with a friend right now, and we are going to find out what is going on soon."

"Okay, be good and be careful."

"I will."

Kyle is trying to get a quickie. "Um, I was wondering if we could, kind of…?"

"You mean finish what we started before you take me over there?"

"Yeah."

He kisses her on the neck and picks her up and carries her to the bed.

"Hey Anna dear?"

"Yes?"

"What did you say?"

"Oh I wanted you to hold me."

"I'm not talking about that."

"What are you talking about? What did I say?"

"You said you were going to bite me."

"No I said I'm not going to bite you."

"But you're a..."

"Never mind. Right now I need to get back to my place."

"But it's 12 o'clock in the afternoon."

"That's cool. I will put on some suntan lotion. Do you have any?"

"No. Besides, I don't think that stuff is going to work anymore."

"It did the first time. You might be right though. I should wait until tonight. I could use a little sleep anyway."

When Anna wakes around 9:00pm she says: "Hey. Good
morning Kyle"
"It's 9:00 o'clock at night. I've already been to the
supermarket and got you some suntan lotion and some
steaks."
"Oh shoot, I have to get to my apartment. Will you take me?"
"Yes. Don't you want me to come with you?"
"Will you?"
"Of course."
They get dressed and drive back to her place. Anna checks
her answering machine. Sure enough, she has a message
from Doctor Page, who wants to check up on her. Anna
listens closely to the message her mother had left about
Donna and Carol. Why did they want her to let them in if
Anna wasn't there? A third message plays. It's Chris,
worried about her because she didn't call him back that night
or the next morning. He also wants to let her know that he
will be in town for a couple of days to visit his cousin Robert

and he reads off the number there. He promises to call her back later. The machine gives up its last message.

"Yo, Anna! You remember us? It looks like the cops are finished at your place. Look, we got unfinished business to solve. We got your little friend just in case you try to run."

"Anna these girls are crazy!" Anna hears the sound of an open hand striking someone.

"Shut the fuck up Bitch!"

"Who is you talking to." Another slap.

"We will kill you, stupid. Look Anna, if you ever want to see your friend again you meet us at Central Park tomorrow night at 10:00pm at the Bank Rock Bridge, and I'm only going to say this once, no cops, and erase this message. Bye."

"Kyle what time is it?"

"It's 9:35. We don't have much time do we?"

"No we don't, but you can't come because you're a cop."

"Yeah but so are you, besides, I can protect you. I can just be your uncle."

Anna doesn't want to disobey the kidnappers' instructions, but she sees the sense in having Kyle along. "Okay come on."

They rush out the door to get in the truck, and drive up to Central Park. They run to the bridge where they meet Donna, who emerged from behind a tree when they passed her, under the lamppost at the end of the bridge. "Hello, you remember me?"

"You! I thought you were dead."

"Yeah well you thought wrong, and I thought I said no cops."

"I'm Anna's uncle. I didn't want her coming out here by herself. Some strong man might attack her."

"Well your uncle is a real gentleman, and he's kind of cute." Donna pinches his cheek.

Carol finally comes up from the rocks on the shore of the stream, holding Brenda at gunpoint. "I heard everything. Hey, that guy is kind of cute. That's your uncle?" Kyle blushes. Carol lets Brenda go. When she frisks him, she finds a badge. "You're a cop?"

"Okay okay, but I'm her best friend, so please don't shoot anyone."

"Oh you mean with this little old .22? I got it off of same boy who tried to rob Donna. The gun is empty now. I was just flashing it so that I could keep better control of Anna's little friend here."

"You bitch, I wish I knew that."

"Shut up Brenda. We and Anna need to have some girl talk about things you don't need to know."

As Carol walks towards Anna, Kyle tries to grab her. She picks him up by the neck with one hand. "If I were you I would get out of the way, got it?"

"Aug acch, yeah, okay."

"Good." As she lets him go, Donna sucker punches Anna on the side of the jaw. "That's for shooting me the first time!" Anna falls face-first toward the frozen concrete path, but gets an arm down and rolls, pops back up and misses Donna with a hard right jab. Carol tackles her, but Anna fights back. She lands a right on Donna, just above the eye, then turns into a big wide left that catches Carol in the mouth and kicks her in the stomach, knocking her on the ground. Donna picks Anna up and slams her into the curved end of the bridge rail.

After that, the two girls quickly overpower Anna. Brenda musters the courage to help her friend. She hits Donna, but Donna just looks at her like she's stupid, before laying the girl right the hell out. Donna pulls out a wooden stake to stab Anna, but Kyle runs up and pulls Donna off and pushes Carol. They redirect their attention at Kyle, but Kyle puts a hand on each of their chests pleading for them to chill. "Wait, wait a minute!"

Carol and Donna look at him, then down at his hand. Kyle notices where he had his hands, unintentionally of course. "Ladies please don't beat me up, and don't kill Anna."
Donna asks, "why not?"
"Because she's the only friend I've got, and she's a good person."
Carol answers, "So? She won't be for long, and if what you say is true, then we have a big problem. Why are we

explaining things to you? Look, get out the way. You're in

over your head."

"Yeah I know that you're… um, upset but here come two

more police officers. So unless to two want to be in the

handcuffs, you girls need to beat it."

The girls look behind them, and sure enough, two street

cops are walking obliviously though the park headed their

way. Kyle lights a cigarette because his hands were shaking,

and turns his head to hide his fear. Cops usually replace it

with anger, but Kyle feels that in this situation it would be

most unwise.

"Okay I'll tell you what; we'll let your friend go. She is very

lucky you are here right now. We only needed to get her

attention. We'll be talking to you soon Anna. Expect a phone

call, and get a damn cell phone already. And I'm not going to

get mad, but don't let my boyfriend catch you feeling us up."

"What do you mean?"

"Your hands."

"Oh, Sorry"

Carol leaves. Donna grab Kyle's butt and asks for 20 bucks, which he gives her so she'll leave. Then Donna gives Kyle a kiss on the cheek and turns to Anna. "Hey your friend is cute. Well, kill you later" and leaves.

Kyle first checks on Anna, as she struggles to get up. "Anna! Are you okay?"

"Yeah. I'll be fine, but you do know that you're on punishment right?"

"Huh? You're okay though right?"

"I got to check on my friend." He helps Anna to her feet. They both check on Brenda, who is just waking up. They help her to her feet. Anna and Kyle let Brenda use them as a crutch. By the looks of things, Brenda was the one that got the worst of it. Anna got her ass whopped. Besides the blood, dirt, and footprints on her shirt, she didn't look too injured. Brenda on the other hand, had a big mouse under her cheek and was walking like a drunk. The two cops walk up and look at Kyle real funny. "Did you beat those girls?"

"No officer he didn't, some girls jumped us."

"Really? Those two girls way up there beat the two of you like that?"

"Yeah but just forget it sir. Were okay."

"Forget it? You sure it wasn't him?"

"I'm sure."

"Okay."

As Kyle and Anna help Brenda to the truck, people look at the girls, then at him and just shake their heads. Once they're in the truck, they drive Brenda to the hospital. "But I'm okay, really."

"No Brenda. We want to make sure."

"Yeah Anna is a vampire she'll be okay, right?"

"She's a what?"

"Um, never mind."

"Brenda he means I stay up all night and sleep all day."

"Oh."

When they get to the hospital, the doctors see the two young ladies right away. Kyle on the other hand is escorted to a small room where he's questioned by two security guards.

"Okay so we are going to ask you one time, what happened to those girls?"

"They got in a fight with two other girls at Central Park."

"Man that's messed up. Can you please turn around for us?"

"Sure, but you know I'm a detective."

"Yeah we believe you. Now can you put your hands behind your back for us?"

"Sure, do you guys want to look in my..."

"Did we say that you could talk yet? Now you got some ID?"

They saw his badge when they checked his ID, apologized and let him explain what happened, at least the part he was willing to tell them.

Brenda gets an ice pack and a dinner. Anna goes to see Dr. Page to get a couple pints of blood to eat. "You know doctor, this stuff isn't that bad, but it isn't that good ether. I don't mind. I can't believe how hungry I am. I sucked all the blood out of maybe ten pounds of meat."

"You've been sucking red meat? Typical rookie mistake. You didn't get more than a couple cc's of blood out of them. What you were getting was myoglobin, an enzyme in muscle tissue. It's like junk food for us. Empty calories. It can be hard to resist sometimes, because it feels so good to be biting into flesh, but don't make a habit of it. Stick to the pint bags."

"I did notice that. It felt so good.'

"Yeah well, after you make your first kill you'll never want to eat this stuff again."

"My first what?"

"You're first kill. Come on you know you're a vampire by now; you're drinking the blood right out of the damn bag right now. By the way, why do you have blood and foot prints all over your shirt?"

"Oh, these two girls beat me up."

"They beat up a vampire? Do you know who they were?"

"One girl name Donna and the other name was Carol."

"Did you say Carol?"

"Yes. You know her?"

"No but that sounds like one of my wife's friends. I will check with her when I get home."

"Thank you doctor."

"You're welcome. Damn, they must have beat your ass. Oh, and you didn't tell anybody our secret did you? "

"The only person that know is my police friend, and he want tell anybody. Second, are you making fun of me?"

"No, it's just that It looks like you were kung fu fighting, and those chicks hit hard as lighting."

She has to laugh, but then she catches herself.

"Yeah okay hardy-har. Well, I'm all set right?"

"Yup, but your friend is going to need an ice pack."

"Okay, thank you doctor."

The first stop after the hospital is Brenda's apartment. She has them buy her a pair of big dark sunglass. She also buys that ice cream that she promised her little brother a couple nights ago. When they arrive at Brenda's place, she bangs on the door and announces herself. "Hey it's me, Brenda, I'm coming in. I have some friends with me." Brenda comes in with Kyle right behind her. Anna is right behind them coming in the door. She feels that shock again.

"Ouch! Shit!"

"Brenda! You know the rules tell your friends no swearing in my house, especially while Brandon is here.

"Sorry mom! Look you guys can't be using profanity, or all of us are going to get our butts kicked."

Anna tries to come in the door again but…

"Ah fuck! Sorry."

"Girl what is wrong with you? And what was that light?"

"Oh yeah, you have to invite her in."

"What? Kyle she knows that she's welcome anytime."

"Tell her."

"Anna come in your invited." Then Anna walks in the door with no further altercation. She silently makes an oath to herself to remember to never forget to get verbal permission before entering someone else's home.

"Anna what was wrong with you? You a vampire?"

Anna freezes. Could it be? Kyle told her already, and she just saw her get shocked, now she knows. Although Brenda's a good friend she is no good at keeping secrets.

"Ha, if you were I wouldn't have had to catch a slug in the eye tonight saving your butt back there?" Anna starts to relax, until Brenda continues her little speech. "Oh yeah, and not to mention the other real ones I had to dodge. I came this close you know, you owe me big time."

Brenda's mother wants to know what was going on.

"What are you talking about Brenda?"

" Just some girl talk mom, that's all."

"No no, Brenda. At first I was mad at you for not coming home, but I know now what happened. Your friend is the lady that got her house shot up last night, and you were there?"

"Um."

"Yeah that's right isn't it? I don't want you around trouble and friends who have enemies like that."

Well that's it, Anna goes from a little tense, to starting to, oh no. Her cheeks turn red with embarrassment. "Well mom she's a cop and she put her life on the line every single day just to make sure that we are safe."

"Yeah you have a good point. I'm sorry Anna. It's just that I worry about my daughter when she's out too late, especially when she doesn't come home or call you know?"

"It's okay, I understand Ms…."

"Yvonne Greenmen."

Anna's friend may have been a little on the clumsy side with secrets sometimes, but she can clean up her mess, and she's a stand-up kind of girl. Brenda goes and gives her little brother that ice cream she promised him. "I got you an ice cream."

"I hate you!"

"What? Why?"

He doesn't answer.

"Well I didn't want to stay out, I got in trouble, and then I got beat up."

"Yeah right."

"You want to see my eye?" Brenda takes off her dark sunglasses. Brandon just looks for a minute in shock.

"See?"

Then Brandon's eyes start getting teary. "No wait don't cry."

"But what's wrong with your eye?"

"I got in a fight."

"Did you win?"

"No, but I'm okay. You know I love you little bro."

"I love you too, don't get in no more fights okay?

"Don't worry I won't. Say, how would you like to chill with me a little more often?"

"Really?"

"Yeah, I will even help mom a lot more with the chores around the house. I'm going to also get a part-time job."

"You will?"

"Yes, I will."

Now Yvonne was listening what Brenda was promising her little brother, and she is overjoyed. Brenda has seen the light. It's like her prayers have been answered, finally. The only thing Yvonne worries about now is those enemies that Brenda may inherit from her police friends if they don't leave her out of it next time. Speaking of time, the time is 3:32 in the morning by Kyle's watch and he reminds everyone that it's time for Anna and him to leave. Brenda is safely delivered to her apartment, well for the most part anyway, and it's time to leave.

4

While in the truck, Anna had asked Kyle to take her home so she could take her shower, change clothes, and get some sleep before the sun came up.

"Yeah it's been a very unusual night, tonight Ms. Davis. You sure you don't want to just pick up some clothes?"

"Yes I'm sure. I need to stay home and collect my thoughts."

"I understand, but what about those bad guys out there? Surely you could use some protection?"

"Well, first of all those were bad girls, and second, my gun is still in the house in my bedroom dresser."

"You are a brave young lady."

"Yeah? Thank you. The way I see it, I'm just tired of all the action right now. Also I don't want you getting hurt trying to protect me."

"I won't get hurt."

"Yeah I saw they really liked you, but they kicked my ass. I don't know if I Should be glad, jealous, or pissed?"

"I wasn't even looking at them like that."

"Maybe not, but how did they feel?"

"Come on don't do this."

"I'm just busting your chops I'm kidding, but all jokes aside, stay away from them. They're dangerous and they would eat you. You already know don't you?"

"Okay. Have a good night or day."

When Kyle pulls over and lets her out, she hesitates a moment and says, "Oh, I almost forgot my hug and kiss." She gives him a hug and a kiss. He kisses her back, but Anna can sense that he is thinking about running at this point. He is in over his head.

"Don't be scared; I won't hurt you. How could you think that? It's me your best friend, the one who always got your back, and that will never change. Okay see you tomorrow." She closes the door of the truck. Kyle waits until she's in her apartment building before he pulls off.

As he's driving back to his place, he stops at a store and buys a Grape Dutch cigar. Outside, he buys a bag of weed from one of the young dealers, gets in the truck and just before he takes off, he calls the young man over "Hey kid, come here for a minute will ya?"

"What? What's up?"

"I don't know how to roll."

"Are you serious? Alright but only this time because you look like you had a rough day."

After the kid rolls the blunt for him, Kyle drives home, parks, and lights it. While the first rush of smoke rolls into his lungs, he puts his seat back.

"Ah man. Five years, just five more years Mr. Miller you can do it, just keep it together."

Then a cop car has pulled up beside him. The police officer gets out of the car and knocks on the window. "Hey! I hate to interrupt your little pow-wow buddy, but I'm going to have to ask you to step out of the car." Kyle rolls down the window, the smoke streaming out of the truck like a river. The police officer has to laugh as he fans the smoke away from his face, attempting to avoid a contact.

"Ha ha ha! Damn, should I call the fire department?"

"If it can happen it will happen, just my luck."

"Sir I'm going to need you to keep your hands on the steering wheel. Wait a minute, is that Kyle Miller?"

"Boy am I done for," he mumbled.

"Oh my gosh it is you. I am so sorry for my vexation Detective sir. I didn't know it was you, and forgive my rudeness it's been a long week. We had an officer stabbed and crash, a boy got his neck broke, witnesses were shot and wounded, I think somebody did a drive by in Central Park or something like that, and a man busted into flame and disappeared. Sir, I think I'm going to call in sick tomorrow."

"You and me both Officer…"

"Hill, Officer Andrew Hill. I work the midnight shift along with Officer Greg and them."

"Oh okay cool. You're not going to say anything about me smoking dope?"

"No sir I didn't see anything. You know, personally I think you're a genius. When you do this line of work, you got to take a load off every once in a while you know, just chill and not take everything so seriously all the time. That's the only way you can stay sane you know?"

"Officer Hill, I know exactly what you're talking about. You want some?"

"Well um, yeah I can take a drag or two, pass that to me, it will get some of the edge off tonight."

Officer Hill takes a puff and breaths, than take another puff, and blows the smoke out with a goofy smile. "Alright thank you detective; I'm not going to take up any more of your relaxation time. I have to get back to work anyway."

Kyle takes the rest of his blunt with him into his building. It starts to hit him as he walks down the hall and gets in the elevator. Vampires… This is insane. There are no vampires, but it would appear that Anna is one, and those two girls. Besides, he had never encountered a woman that strong, or a man for that matter. If she'd wanted to, she could have snapped his neck with one hand. Apparently there have been vampires the whole time he's been alive. What world has he been living in?

The elevator ride leaves Kyle feeling disoriented. As he enters his apartment, he focuses only on turning the key to the door. The walk across his floor feels like a walk on the surface of a strange planet, and he's never sure if the surface beneath his feet will give way with each step. When he finally reaches the couch, Kyle takes off his shoes and coat and finishes what's left of his blunt.

"So, I was sucked into this job 15 years ago, my ex-wife tried to suck all my money out of my wallet. My best friend, who is now also my girlfriend, is now a little bloodsucker. Somebody once told me that our friends are all we've got, so I guess I'm going to have to suck it up and deal with what's in front of me. I guess I can use one more sick day this week. It's 4:30 in the morning? I'm off today and I still feel like I'm on duty."

Kyle calls Anna to tell her he made it in safely, and she's

glad, then he sets his alarm clock for 8:00am so he could get up and lie in the morning. He gets in the bath and then goes to bed.

Anna has also taken her bath and got into her bathrobe. She checks her voice messages and erases the old messages, except for the one that Chris left her. She calls his cell phone right away.

"Hello, Chris?"

"Yeah it's me."

"I am so sorry I couldn't get a hold of you until now. I hear that you're up here for a couple of days."

"Yeah I am, but you wouldn't care about a thing like that."

"Yes I do, but my house got shot up the night before last."

"That was you?"

"Yeah that was me."

"You made the news you know, are you alright?"

"I'm okay, but my girlfriend had to dodge a couple of bullets. She did catch a black eye, and I caught a beat down."

"Who did this?"

"Two other girls."

"Damn girl, you got beef like that?"

"Yeah I'm afraid so, but I'm tired right now, I'll call you tomorrow night."

"Okay."

" I promise. You can come by tomorrow too."

"While you got beef with those gangster killer chicks, I don't think so."

"What?"

"I'm just kidding, get some sleep. Call me tomorrow okay?"

"Okay."

Then they both hang up, and Anna goes to bed for the night. She sleeps in peace, in peace until the phone rings and awakes her around one o'clock in the evening. She hears the answering machine click in, her own voice broadcasts across the room, and then the beep. Anna grabs the phone

"Hello, I'm here hello."

"Good afternoon Officer Davis, this is Officer Swanson, Hailey Swanson. I'm just calling to make sure you're okay. So how are you doing? Are you okay?"

"Yes, and thank you for calling. Sorry I've been out for 6 days now."

"Hey don't even worry about it. You have been through a lot of shit lately, if I do say so myself. First you get attacked in the alley by a gang and barley escape with your life. You found the strength to run and get away before crashing the car. Then after you get out of the hospital, someone comes after you again and shoots up your place?"

"Yeah I know right? It's ridiculous."

"No it's crazy, and personally, I'm surprised that you're not in a nut house somewhere along whit your situation. That, or a vigilante. You're a brave and strong woman Ms. Davis, and I admire you. Take as much time as you need, we won't hold anything against you."

"When I come back to work, can I get the night shift?"

"Sure, 11:30pm to 7:30am. Ok?"

"No. I mean more like 9:00pm to 500am."

"What? Maybe you did go a little crazy."

"I'm serious."

"Why? You know shifts don't go like that."

"Just trust me. I have to be at work after sundown, and be back home before sunrise."

"Well, okay I will try my best to make that happen, no promises. I will talk to you later. Glad you're okay. Bye-bye."

As soon as Anna hangs up the phone, it rings again.

"Hey Anna dear this is your mom. You picked up pretty quickly; you must have been sitting right next to the phone."

"Hi mom."

"You sound tired."

"I am, I've been up all night."

"Honey I'm coming over there. Something is wrong and you are not telling me."

"Nothing is wrong. I just been hanging out with my friend all night, and I need to sleep."

"You've been just hanging out with your friends all night? Well get some sleep dear. Call me as soon as you wake up."

"All right, I will."

"Ok bye-bye."

After they hang up, Anna says to herself if one more person calls her, she will turn off the ringer. Then she goes back to bed and sleeps like a rock. She wakes up at

10:30pm and immediately calls her parents, as promised.

Then she calls Brenda. "Hey what's up?"

"Hi Anna, how are you doing?"

"I'm doing good. Hey are you single?

"Yeah, but I shouldn't be right?"

"I have a guy for you if you're interested."

"What? I'm not looking for a boyfriend right now."

"Okay, but he's a good guy you know."

"Then why don't you go out with him? As a matter of fact,

who is this guy anyway?"

"His name is Chris, and I spoke with him over the phone. He

came all this way to see me from Rochester, but I haven't

had any time to pay attention to him. Plus I'm kind of

messing around with Kyle."

"Really, damn that's messed up."

"I know, I'm such a bitch for that right?"

"No not at all, but you have to tell him. Don't lead him on if

you're not interested."

"I have an idea."

"What's that?"

"Let's call him on the three way."

"Wait a minute. What's his name again? Is he white or black? Does he drive?"

Anna had already clicked over to call him.

"Hello."

"Hey, I told you I would call you back."

"About time, I was starting to think you straight up forgot about me."

"No, I didn't forget about you."

"Well, how you been babygirl? How was your night out? You never told me. Well, besides the attack on your home and all?"

"It was good. Me and my friends had a very exciting night."

"Well that's a lot of excitement for one night."

"Yeah I know."

"You deserve a little R&R. Can I come by? I will bring you a rose, and run you a bubble bath."

"Really? You sure you not just trying to get some?"

"Hey, don't worry about that. I just want to hold you. If you "want to that's cool, and if you don't, that's cool too."

"Ooh, Anna he's adorable."

"What the! Who is that?"

"My name is Brenda, and I've heard some good things about you."

"Anna you got me on the 3 way?"

"She's a police officer, you should be lucky that she doesn't have you on a walky-talky."

"Wait a minute! Anna you're a cop?"

"Yes, and I hope you don't hold that against me, as I don't hold my girlfriend's big mouth against her."

"Ah girl I am so sorry, but I figured you told him. It's not a bad job."

"Yeah Anna. Why did you feel that you couldn't tell me that?"

"Because, how does this sound? Hi my name is Anna Davis. I like long walks on the beach, and I work for the NYPD and... hello, hello are you still there, hello? Not very good."

"Ok I get your point. I kind of know you now, so you don't have to worry about me running like Goldilocks."

"Anna can I ask him?"

"Ask him what? Oh, sure go ahead."

"Can I get your number Chris? You know, so I can call you when I get bored?"

"Ah, this is a test right?"

"Nope. Brenda is serious, y'all can swap numbers, I won't get mad or hold it against you."

So Brenda and Chris swap numbers while Anna is trying to slide off of the three way. She feels that Chris had come this far just to see her and she wouldn't have time for him. Not because she doesn't like him. In fact, she knows in the back of her head that she will kick herself later, but it's hard to be a good friend if you're too selfish to consider other people. She gets off the phone so that Brenda can talk to him, but in the back of her head, there's the urge to go back and see or maybe even sample, what she's just missed out on.

"Ok guys I have to go for now."

"Okay."

"Alright, y'all ladies don't be strangers now."

Then Anna clicks back over and it's just Anna and Brenda on the line.

"So what do you think?"

"Yeah I think I like him."

"I knew you would, he's a nice catch, but whatever you do, don't tell him that... you know. Or he will hate me."

"Oh you good girl, your secrets are safe with me, like always."

"Like always? Brenda you have been so clumsy with half of all my secrets lately. I am in so much trouble."

"No you're not. I didn't know that you didn't want him to know you're a police officer. I'm your friend. Come on now."

"I know. Just be careful what you tell him about me okay? You'll be dropping dime on me without realizing it."

Anna gets another call. "Hold on okay?

"Hello."

"Anna how are you doing tonight?"

"I'm doing okay, I'm on the phone with Brenda."

"Can you come over?"

"What? Yeah right. Last night you couldn't get away from me fast enough. What do you have to say for yourself?

"Well ah, umm..."

"Oh that was so funny! You know I'm not mad at you. Well maybe a little. Hold on a minute, I can't leave her hanging. "Brenda."

"Who is that?"

"It's Kyle, he wants me to come over."

"You're going to get you some?"

"Oh yeah, you know it."

"Alright then, I'll let you go ahead then. Have fun, and leave him whipped."

"Girl if you only knew. Okay, good night."

"Good night."

"Kyle?"

"Hello."

"Yeah I'm on the way, let me get dressed."

Anna has just taken her shower early this morning, but still.

She goes to the bathroom and freshens up, and puts on some Apple perfume, a comfortable pair of blue shorts and a white tummy tuck shirt, and a pair of Nikes. Then she puts on her bathrobe. Something reminds Anna to grab her gun just in case she runs into Carol and Donna again. On the drive over to Kyle's, her intuitions start kicking in, the weirdest felling she ever had. It frightens her, and at the same time soothes her. About half way to Kyle's place she hears a masculine voice behind her.

"Well hello there."

Anna screams, and almost loses control of the car as she skids into the curb.

"You're a hard woman to get a hold of. Please don't crash, I don't have on my seat belt."

She opens her eyes, wider and wider, and screams again. Then she opens the door while leaving the car in drive, and tries to jump out. The man grabs her by her robe and pulls her back in.

"Look at me!"

"Who are you? What do you want?"

Wait a minute, oh no! It's that man with the dark brown hair she met in that alley. Not him! No way!

"Calm down Anna."

She pushes his face away with one hand, while at the same time reaching in her pocket for something with the other. The man grabs her hand. When she pulls out her gun and he grabs the gun too and rips it away from her before she can fire it. He hops up in the front seat and bashes her head on the steering wheel.

"Hey! What are you doing with that?" He yells. "Give it here!" Anna screams as her head hits the horn in the center of the wheel. The man puts an arm around her and pulls her close against him. "Now come here and calm down! I said I'm not going to hurt you!"

"You just did, you damn brute."

"Oh, well ok. I mean from now on. Like I said, you're a hard woman to get a hold of."

"Oh yeah? Well those psycho ass girls of yours didn't seem to have a hard time."

"Wait a minute. You already spoke to them?"

"Did I? They spoke to me all right. They tried to kill me."

"Donna has quite a bad temper sometimes, but I don't think they want to kill you. Carol might, because you know too much."

"Well I'm pretty sure of it. They even kidnapped my friend to get my attention."

She pulled over and puts the car in park. "It's clear that those girls want me dead."

"Do you think that I want you dead?"

"I don't know. I guess not. Why are you here?"

"You have seen too much, and I am here to offer you a choice."

Then he bites her. Anna's eyes open wide with surprise. When she realizes what he's doing, she starts to struggle against him, but she can't stop him. To her surprise, she doesn't want to. Just as suddenly, he stops.

"You didn't tell me that you were already a vampire. You

turned at the hospital that night or sometime this week didn't

you? This means that I am your direct elder. "

"What?"

"According to the Council Empires."

"I'm hungry."

"I think I know what's going on now; Carol and Donna both

want to kill you."

"Really? I didn't notice."

"Oh, sorry I didn't believe you. Now it makes since. Besides

Donna having a ridiculously bad temper, Carol doesn't seem

to like you for some reason."

"Tell me something that I don't know."

"When I bit you, your blood didn't taste human this time.

Your blood also doesn't taste fully like a vampire yet. That's

weird, but you're new so whatever. I have to train you."

"You can tell that I'm a vampire?"

"Yes I can. Now your friend isn't very smart, I'm talking

about the one who couldn't keep his hands off of my woman.

I should kill him."

"She told you? He didn't mean any harm."

"No I suppose not. She would have put him in his place if he angered her. That much I know."

"Please don't hurt him."

"Fine. Can I meet him though?"

"Umm, can you stop those crazy ass girls from trying to kill us please?"

"Funny. You're trying to shift the conversation. First of all, those girls aren't trying to kill your female friend, or your lover."

"My lover? Okay you got me, but who talks like that?"

"Carol and Donna are just trying to kill you."

"I know! Can you stop them?" She yelled"

"So that's why Carol sent me to the hospital that night. She knew you were not there. Oh she is slick. Well, I can order Donna to leave you alone, and I can talk to Carol and see if I can calm her down."

"If you can order Donna, then how come you can't order that evil ass girlfriend of yours to do the same?"

"Because she's my direct elder, and she could actually order me to kill you."

"What? Oh shit."

"But she's my lady. She doesn't like to pull rank on me like that. Perhaps every once in a blue moon or so."

"Rank?"

"Oh come on you know, like the army. If she orders me to do something and I don't do it, if she tells the council then I could get in big trouble."

"Oh, I understand. Wait a minute, the who? Who is the council? You mean that there is an empire of blood suckers running around?"

"Um, you know what? Never mind that right now. I will talk to Carol and ask her not to kill you."

"How comforting."

"Huh? I can calm her down don't worry. If she gets all crazy or something, I will give you the heads up."

"I'm hungry."

"Okay, I will take the wheel. You hop on the passenger side while I get you something to eat."

"Okay."

"By the way, my name is James."

"I know. I remember one of the girls calling your name back in the alley."

He gives her a little weird look, but takes the wheel while she moves over to the passenger side. They pull up to a young woman coming from the corner store.

"Hey lady! You in the black fur coat!"

"Yes?"

"Can you come here for a minute, I need your help!"

"What's wrong! You know I don't know you, so I can't really talk to you."

"Please lady it's my sister. She's having trouble breathing."

"Oh no, is there something I can do to help?"

"Yes. I need you to help her out of the car, and I will call an ambulance."

"Okay I will."

She runs over to the door and tries to open it, but the door is locked. He hits the button to unlock it while she tries the handle a second time, but the lady dashes into the store, screaming at the top of her lungs.

"Can I get some help out here? These people are in trouble,

and I don't know what to do!"

       Ten people run out of the store to give assistance. James is in shock to see how badly his little lie has backfired.

"Um, guys! I'm just going to go ahead and take her to the hospital, but thank you for coming out."

He drops the car into drive and punches the gas. Anna is still complaining that she's hungry; she's getting weak and even turning whitish blue.

"Please feed me."

"Okay I will give you some of my blood, hold on."

"No wait, take me to the hospital."

"You want me to take you to the hospital?"

"Yes"

"That's too far right now."

"Where is Tops?"

"It's around the corner, why?"

"Take me."

James thinks this is the worst idea ever, but he still takes her. When he pulls up in the parking lot, she tells him to pull up to the front of the store. Anna staggers out of her car.

"I will be back in 5 minutes"

"What are you going to do?"

She doesn't answer. She just staggers into the store, though the sliding doors. James feels bad: he did drink a lot of her blood, and she probably was already hungry before he bit her. Wait a damn minute! Oh Shit! He did not just let this young, brand new, insanely hungry vampire in a supermarket full of mortals. If she feeds on someone in the supermarket, it will be in front of everybody. It would make the news, and that wouldn't be good, and if she's captured, that would be even worse. That would expose their existence. The council would surely want to catch the guy responsible for that. It certainly wouldn't be Anna. Let Carol tell it, according to her, the council will probably just kill all four of them together. The empire will probably knock off the head of the American council to protect other councils. Who knows? The way Carol tells it, vampire hunters would come and hunt and kill them all indiscriminately, or by something even worse, slayers. Carol's never talked much about slayers. She once said that you would have to be pretty damn messy, or powerful and bad to get the attention of a slayer. Although there are less than a hand full, if you manage to get one after you, just run. Run and pray, and run some more. Leave everything behind and get out of that country. That's all she's explained about them.

Anyway, all he knows right now is that he had better go and get that girl. He puts the car in park and turns off the engine. But as he opens the door and puts his foot on the ground, he hears, "hey buddy! What the hell do you think you're doing?" A cop is shouting at him.

"What now?"

"Go park that car! You're not special!"

That was close. He finds a parking spot just to shut that clueless cop up.

In the supermarket, Anna staggers her way to the meat department, and boy does she seem to like those T-bone steaks. She starts chewing the red out of them, right there in front of everyone. "Mommy why is that lady eating the meat raw?"

"Honey umm, some people don't know that you're suppose to cook."

"But…"

"Come on honey let's leave the nice lady alone."

In less than a minute she's the center of attention, and she's also on her third steak. A butcher comes out yelling with a meat cleaver still in his hand.

"Look lady I know you're crazy, so I'm going to give you a break. I have spent a lot of time chopping up that meat. You're wasting my food! Just stop!"

Still chewing, she looks at him and says. "I will pay you back, now go get me some ribs or something please."

"Are you stupid?"

"Now!"

"Oh shit! What the fuck! That is it, I'm punching out. I've got to get out of here!"

When he's gone, Anna starts on the ribs. She finds that the

pork ribs taste terrible. She spit it out the first taste. Beef ribs taste much better. Two security guards and a man in suit have arrived on the scene.

"Ma'am what the, what are you doing?"

She ignores them, and everybody in the supermarket, who were still staring, and wondering the same thing.

"Look ma'am, first of all you're suppose to cook that, and second, you didn't pay for that."

Still chewing, she looks at them. She grabs one more T-bone steak and puts it in a plastic bag for later. They were juicy.

"Damn it lady. I'm going to have to ask you to put down those meats"

"BUT I'M HUNGRY!"

She roars, her teeth like a lion, and her bathrobe soaked in blood. She looks so irritated to be distracted from her meal. Everybody gasps. The two security guards put their hands on their holsters and the man in the suit reaches inside his coat. One of the security guards gets on his walky-talky and says what everybody is thinking. "I need somebody to get me an exorcist up here, right now."

"Say again? Say what! Over."

"I said an exorcist! Or maybe a dart gun and some holy water, and an ambulance!"

"What? Don't play games over the radio, over."

"I'm serious, we have a woman in Aisle 9 who has been possessed by the Devil."

"Then get her some chocolate or something, over and out."

Okay, it's clear that the head of the watch team has more important things to deal with than another unruly little lady in a supermarket. At this point they don't know what to do. By now Anna has snapped back to her senses, realizing that she's in an extremely awkward position, and in the middle of a public place. People are staring at her with their chins on the floor, and there is no way to get the look of disbelief off of their faces. So she does what's in her mind, the only sensible thing left to do. She grabs the last three steaks laying out, puts them in the bag, and starts walking out of the store, fast, saying, "Sorry everybody. I was so hungry that I couldn't wait to cook. I will send somebody with the money to pay for the food. So please don't call the police. Just give me 24 hours, for now I have to go."

She continues walking until she's out of the store. People stare at the brown, bone-dry meat she has left the floor, that used to be red. People stare at her, but nobody stops her or even gets in her way.

5

Back at the car, James is panicking. It has been only seven

minutes since Anna walked into the supermarket, but

knowing how hungry she was, and the fact that she has only

been a vampire for only a few days, is not helping any. As he

comes around the corner, he has the urge to just drive off,

and ditch the car a couple blocks away, but then he realizes

that he's acting in a panic. His head clears. "What the hell

am I doing? I got to go get that girl." As he pulls over to the

curb again, a knock on the window startles him.

"Hi, I'm back"

It's Anna. He opens the door and she gets in. She has blood

all over her bathrobe, and a bag of bloody meats in her

hand. James' eyes get big and his mouth opens wide.

"Hi, I told you I wouldn't be long."

"What the! You ate somebody right in the supermarket?" His voice is rising to a hysterical scream.

"No, but let's get out of here."

"Yeah, that might be a good idea."

So he puts the car into gear and starts driving. As they pull away, sure enough, the people who were in the store start coming outside in curiosity to see where that crazy lady is going. A woman in the crowd saw Anna jump in the car, but can't get a good enough look to identify the car as James pulls out of the lot and races out of the area.

"Anna are you insane?" He is yelling.

"No. Why?"

"Look at you."

"Yeah I know, I lost my head."

"Whatever you did back there, got you all covered in blood, from your teeth to your bath robe."

"Yes I know, I know."

"Well do you also know that you are going to make the News?"

"Really? Oh shit you're probably right. This is all your fault

James! You took too much and left me starving!"

"Hey cool it bloodbath lady! I remember offering you some of my blood."

"No. Never mind just take me home."

"Oh right. Well it's your car, so you can have back the driver's seat. Just let me pull over so I can get out right here."

He pulls the car over and gets out.

"Oh and by the way, I will let my girls know that you're one of us now. You know, so they can stop trying to kill you."

"Okay thank you. I think."

What an asshole. That or a beautiful, barbaric screw up of a man. Did he just rudely invade his way into her life, have her for dinner, and flip her whole life upside down, again? Then just leave her with "well I will tell the girls that you're a vampire so they don't kill you" and thinks he did her a favor? She slides over to the driver's seat, takes the wheel, and heads for home. "I can't believe that guy after all that, called me the bloodbath lady, yeah very funny."

The fact that she is wearing a blood soaked bathrobe

makes her laugh, and the other fact, is that the car smells like leather and raw hamburger meat, this makes laugh even harder.

Anna is at home, she is looking at the clock beside her bed. "Twelve-thirty in the morning, I was supposed to be at Kyle's an hour ago. I really got to get me a cell phone." She calls him up.

"Hey Kyle, I'm sorry that I kept you waiting. I had a run-in with the guy who bit me the first time in the alley."

"What happened? Did he hurt you?"

"Not really, but he bit me again."

"What do you mean he bit you again?

"I mean he bit me! Again!"

"Okay okay. Then what?"

"Then he had taken a lot of my blood and I got really hungry. I mean starving. We didn't have time to go to the hospital so he drove me to Tops."

"You're a vampire, what were you going to do at the hospital?"

"I was going to pick up a couple of pints."

"Oh I see. So let me guess, you ate some of those steaks and some lamb chops at the store?"

"Yeah well, some steaks and some beef ribs. How did you know?"

"That's what you did over at my place. Well what else did the guy want?"

"He wanted to make sure that I was a vampire so that his girls didn't have to kill me."

"You didn't kill anybody did you?"

"No. I didn't kill or bite anybody. You know that I wouldn't do that."

"Sorry, but I had to ask."

"Gee thanks."

"Are you sure that your okay? I'm coming over there."

"Yeah that might not be a good idea right now."

"You sure? Why not?"

"Because I thought I would surprise you by coming to see you in something sexy, and I wore my new robe over it to keep myself warm and comfortable. Now, I'm covered in blood because I had a hunger attack in the super market in front of everybody."

"Well I know you, I understand, well at least I'm trying to. This is getting pretty damn weird."

"I'm sorry, I don't know what to do."

"It's ok it's not your fault, you just got caught up in some BS we didn't know really existed."

"Yeah I know, and I'm scared."

"I'm coming over, if it's ok with you."

"Ok, but don't get scared because, right now I look like the bloodbath lady."

"I will be there in fifteen minutes."

Anna takes off her blood soaked robe and puts it in a plastic bag, then throws the bag in the garbage. There is no way on God's green earth that she's going to get that red robe white ever again. After that she unlocks the door for Kyle, grabs a change of clothes and hops in the shower.

As soon as she steps out of the shower, she hears the doorbell.

She buzzes Kyle in. "Come on up, my door's unlocked!"

Then she retreats to the bathroom, where she dries off and dresses. She hears footsteps in her living room and Kyle calling in to her, "Yeah it's me. I'm in the living room."

"Okay! I just got out of the shower; I'll be out in a minute."

She comes out to greet him in a pair of Maroon sweat pants, and a black tank top shirt. "Hi Kyle, I'm glad you came."

"I was getting worried about you."

"Thank you, yeah I'm okay. I have to take care of my clothes real quick."

She puts her shorts in the hamper, but has to toss the shirt in the garbage with the bathrobe.

"Well I'm glad you're ok. I have to get back home because I got to get up for work in the morning."

"You can sleep here, you know."

"Well, only if you promise to get me up early enough tomorrow for work."

"I will. What time you get up?"

"I've got to be in at 7:00am. Wake me at five."

"I will. Now come to bed, I want you to hold me."

As they lay in bed, Anna presses herself up against him.

Kyle laughs, a little nervously. "What are you doing?"

"Nothing, you want to do something?"

The hours fly by. It seems like Anna is just drifting off to sleep one minute, and the next the alarm clock is buzzing. It's 5:00 in the morning.

"Kyle. Honey, it's time to get up."

"Huh?"

"It's 5:00am, you told me to wake you up for work."

"Okay, oh yeah thank you."

Kyle drags himself out of the bed and goes to the bathroom to wash up and brush his teeth. Lucky for him, Anna has an extra toothbrush. When he comes out he gives her a hug and kiss, then gets ready to head out.

"Will you make it?"

"I'll be fine. I've had almost three hours' sleep, and I'm not even hung over. Just a little whipped." Anna gives him a smile and a kiss.

"I'll cook something for you when you get back."

"Really? Thank you, you're the best."

Alone in the apartment, Anna is restless. She'd be asleep around this time. The sun will be up soon. Not knowing exactly what to do with herself, she fries some chicken wings, cooks some mixed vegetables, and some macaroni and cheese. It would be delicious, if she could eat it. She walks back into the bedroom. She wishes she could call someone, but it's too early, so she reluctantly sits on the bed and lies down.

An hour later the phone wakes her. "Hello?"

"Girl wake your butt up!"

"Brenda? What's wrong? What's going on?"

"Just get up and put it to Channel 4."

So Anna gets out of bed, puts the food she cooked in the fridge real quick, and turns on the television.

"Did you turn on the news yet?"

"Yes, I just did."

"What do you see?"

"Holy shit!!"

"We're back with that story about the ghoul at Gristede's. Apparently, someone was a little too much into the Halloween spirit late last night. A young woman had walked into the supermarket last night at about 11:45 and got her grub on. Witnesses say that she came in the store, went straight to the meat department, and started chewing on some ribs and steaks --no salt, no pepper, no cooking." In the grainy video, her face wasn't recognizable, but it was clear what she was doing. Was that really her? Watching herself, Anna felt unnerved and curled up and hugged her knees while the anchors made inane jokes about her.

"Anna I know that was you. What were you thinking? Are you really going nuts or something?"

"No I just had a hunger attack."

"A hunger attack? What?"

"Brenda if I tell you something, can you keep it a... never mind."

"What is it? I know I have a big mouth about little stuff some times, but if you tell me something that is between me and you."

"Ok um, I'm a..."

Anna's phone beeps.

"Hold on one second Brenda. Someone is on the other line."

She clicks over.

"Hello."

"Anna! Is everything all right?"

"Yes, hi mom. Why you ask me like that?"

"Turn on the TV and turn it to channel 4."

"I know, I see. I'm watching it right now."

"Anna dear, I have a question to ask you, and don't tell me a story. Is that you on TV?" She didn't answer. "Well is it?"

"No mom it's not."

"Bullshit Pumpkin that is you!"

"Dad?"

"Yeah! We're both sitting here watching you on TV. They hid your face a little bit but we know our daughter when we see her."

"Hold on I have my girlfriend on the other line."

"Hello Brenda?"

"It's me. I'm still here."

"It's my mom and Dad."

"What are they doing up so early?"

"The same thing you're doing."

"Watching you on the News?"

"Yup."

"Do they know it's you on the News?"

"Yup they sure do. They said they know me when they see me."

"Wow you're going to hear it."

"I know, can I call you back? As a matter of fact can you come over?"

"Sure, I want you to tell me what's going on. Besides, I've got to admit that I don't want to miss this."

"Thank you."

"No problem. You're the only 5-0 I would do anything for. You know what, for a cop you sure…"

"Thank you. See you when you get here, bye."

"Hello Mom, Dad, let me tell you what happened."

"Oh sweet heart you're a little late for that."

"Yeah Pumpkin we see what you're going to tell us, and what you would not tell us."

"Mom, Dad, I'm sorry that you saw that. Please don't freak out when I tell you what I am now."

"Don't worry honey, we already know and it's okay."

"You know?"

"Yes Pumpkin we know what you've turned into." Anna paused in silence while wanting to hear their answer. "A fucking nut job, but you're still our little girl and we are going to get though this, as a family."

"I'm not a nut job. I'm a vampire."

"Donald Anna thinks she's a vampire."

"Pumpkin, vampires aren't real."

"Come over and I will prove it."

"You know what sweetie, that's a good idea."

"Yeah Pumpkin, your mother and I are going to get dressed

and stop over to help you find your marbles."

Fifteen minutes later, Anna hears the doorbell.

"Hold on I'm coming!"

Anna hits the buzzer, and unlocks the door. She has to swiftly step to the side before Brenda opens the door. The sun coming in the front door casts a narrow beam into her apartment.

"Hey Anna it's me. Why are all of your curtains down? Here, let me open some of these curtains for you so we can get some light in here."

"Brenda no!"

"Whoa! What the heck jumped into you?"

"I'm sorry. I didn't mean to yell at you, but please don't open those curtains."

"Ok but you're acting like a vampire or something. You know, up all night sleep all day. You're even scared of sunlight, does it hurt your eyes or something?"

"Brenda?"

"Yes?"

"I am a vampire."

"See, you even agree."

"No I'm serious. I'm a vampire."

"You're something but you're not a vampire. They don't exist."

"I can show you."

"Okay got ahead, but don't bite me because I'm not into the kinky stuff"

"Okay." Anna grabs Brenda by the collar of her shirt with one hand and lifts Brenda straight up in the air with no problem.

"Wow, I had no idea you were that strong."

"I told you, I'm different now."

"Ok put me down. How long have you been a vampire?"

"Ever since I got bit that night and almost died from loss of blood."

"So those two girls are the ones from that night in the alley?"

"Yes, I shot the Blond. The other girl knocked me on the ground, and the guy bit me. You never met him but, he wants me turned and the girls want me dead."

"Well that explains everything, but you do know that this is a little hard to... never mind, ok does Kyle know?"

"Yes, I told him the night it happened. He didn't believe me though, until later."

"Was he ok with it?"

"No he freaked out at first, but he seems to be ok with it now."

The doorbell rings again. Anna buzzes her parents in and then walks toward the door to open it and steps to the side. However, before she can do this, her father opens the door wide, and Anna is caught like a deer in the headlights.

"Hi sweetie we made it."

"Ahhhhh!!"

She lets out a scream that could break windows in her apartment. Brenda, who has already been briefed on what is going on, pushes her out of the sunlight just as she starts to smoke a little. Both parents watch in awe. Donald's chin hits the floor, while Carrie, just hits the floor. Donald catches her before she hits her head and carries her to the couch, and goes back to help the other little lady pick up Anna. They help her up and try the get her to bed until they can figure out what to do.

"I'm okay, I'm okay. Take me to the kitchen. I have food."

They take her to the kitchen and she opens the refrigerator door, pulls out the raw steaks, and catches herself. Her canine teeth have grown long and sharp and she's about to eat right in front of them.

"Excuse me for a minute; can you go in the living room in a minute."

"Are you going to be alright Pumpkin?"

"Yes, I will be. Thanks Dad."

"We'll be watching the News. Come on in here with us when you're done eating."

They leave her alone in the kitchen. Brenda and the Davises introduce themselves, which was as normal as it was going to get today.

Then the phone rang.

"Anna can I answer it?"

"Sure Brenda, go ahead."

"Hello Anna?"

" No this is Brenda. But she's here hold on. Anna It's Kyle!"

"Here I come!"

As she comes out of the kitchen, her father says "Pumpkin you've got Kool-Aid running down your chin."

"Oops. Sorry about that."

Anna grabs a paper towel to wipe it off, and gets on the phone. Brenda and Donald just look at each other.

"Anna I've got something important to tell you... That wasn't you on TV was it?"

"Yeah it was me."

"Oh no!"

"What do you mean oh no?"

"I mean oh no! Did you watch the News this morning?"

"Yes, and we are about to watch it again in 30 minutes."

"We? What do you mean?"

"Brenda and my mom and dad are here, they knew it was

me. Brenda woke me up first, and we are all here."

"Wow really? Well go ahead and just put me on the speaker phone, unless you don't want them to hear what I have to say."

"No, I don't want to keep any more secrets from them."

"Hello everybody, my name is Kyle Miller, and I'm a good friend of Anna's."

"Don't you mean boyfriend Mr. Kyle? You don't want to hurt Anna's feelings do you?"

"Yes I mean boyfriend, and no Brenda, I wouldn't want to hurt Anna's feelings. I just wasn't sure if she was ready to let anybody know yet."

"It's okay. I thought you were scared. So it's official then: we are a couple."

"That's great news, you just made me a happy man, but I'm afraid I have a little bad news."

"Wait a minute; you're going out with my daughter? How old are you? And what do you do for a living?"

"Sir I'm 42, and I'm a detective in the Manhattan Police

Department. Can we talk about that stuff a little later sir?"

Anna interrupts. "What's wrong Kyle? What happed?"

"I have some bad news, a little bit of good news, and some real bad news. Someone in the department got some of the video tape outside of the store, so they investigated it, and they found out that it was you."

"Oh no! Well what's the good news?"

"When I found out, I had to do a lot of convincing. Well actually, I just bought you some time to come up with a good story as to what is going on with you. Still, everybody in your precinct had your back. We told the News that you were just some College student on a wild dare by one of the fraternity groups. They offered to pay for you tuition for the semester for that stunt. I know a couple of people who are contacts for the local stations, and they passed it along anonymously."

"Wow, you guys covered for me like that?"

"We sure did Ms. Davis."

"Thank you, I was starting to get worried. You guys are the best."

"Oh you're welcome, but you're not off the hook."

"What do you mean?"

"Your captain was talking about you getting fired, but we reminded him that you're one of our best. Then he talked about suspending you."

"I'm suspended?"

"No you're not suspended. He just talked about it. We reminded him that you've been through a lot. I mean, you're out on comp and you are still getting shot at and treated. I made sure that he took that into consideration."

"Well that's good, what did he say?"

"Um, you don't work there anymore."

Anna is silent.

"Hello, are you still there?"

"That's terrible! That's real messed up!"

"Well actually that's still the good news. The captain said that when you get off comp that you're going to have a choice. They think that you have lost your mind, and there's an ordinary disability package together for you. Pumpkin you're about to get crazy checks."

"Is that true Kyle?"

"Actually, yes it is. Now the second option of your choice is that, when you come back from comp, you are going to be re-assigned to all paid detail work. You're going to be working in banks, the stock exchange, and different job sites."

Brenda is laughing for a moment, before asking Kyle what he thinks.

"You mean Anna's going to be a rent-a-cop?"

"Yeah Brenda a rent-cop like you said. It's not funny Brenda, she'll still be police."

"Kyle come on. You know that's some boring stuff, I will hate it."

"Well unless we can convince personnel that you're didn't go crazy, or have some kind of breakdown, then those are your options. Hey, it could be worse. You could be working behind a desk somewhere."

"Yeah that's true."

"Now are you ready for the real bad news?"

"What? No freaking way?"

"Well, here goes anyway."

"No wait. Hold on a minute." Anna sits down.

"Ok I'm ready, go ahead."

"All right, a half an hour before the police came to the store, an unknown team of investigators confiscated all of the video footage inside of the store."

"What do you mean an unknown team?"

"I mean that we don't know these people, or where they are from."

"I thought the NYPD got the tapes."

"Yes but only outside of the store. When we arrived, the managers told us that the police had already showed up a half hour before we did, and the store gave it up without any questions. We don't have a record or video surveillance of any of them before us."

"You're right. That doesn't sound good at all."

Then the news comes on and Anna, Brenda, and Donald sit down. Carrie is just getting up, still trying to grasp the fact that everything around her is starting to look like an episode of the Outer Limits. Kyle lets them go, and they all watch the News. The story is updated with a note that sources have informed them that the incident was likely a fraternity prank. They run the footage again, of course. Brenda says, "By tomorrow, that'll be set to a dance beat and have a million hits on YouTube." Anna knows she's right. She laughs along with everyone else, but she's working her mind around the men who impersonated NYPD detectives in New York City, the men somewhere out there who have her image.

6

Anna is alone in her apartment. Her parents left in the late afternoon. Brenda has gone home, attempting to keep a promise that she had made to herself. It was to spend a little more time at home with her mother and little brother. Come to mention it, little Brandon has been doing better in school the last couple of days with her home more, so Brenda has started to realize that she is needed by more than just her friends.

Anna respects it, and she is proud of Brenda for that. She even gives Brenda a ride down to her place. Then she drives to the hospital to see if Doctor Page was there so she could talk to him for a minute. When Anna gets to the hospital, she learns that Doctor Page has just got there 15 minutes before her. "Good," she thinks, and asks to speak to him. To Anna's surprise, he has the time to come down and speak to her right away. "Hi Anna, it's nice to see you. What's up?"

 "I'm hungry and I need a couple of pints."

"Oh no problem. I'm glad to see that you're finally eating. Where is your purse? You don't expect to carry pints out of here with your hands do you?"

"Yeah you're right. I didn't think about that when I came up here."

"Well, we have plastic bags."

"Okay, it will have to do."

So Anna ends up walking out of the hospital with twelve pint bags inside of that big black garbage bag that Dr. Page had given her, and it looks tacky, but it works. She gets in the car and drives home and takes all of the food out of her freezer and sets it on the table. She takes out three pint bags to eat, then puts the rest in the freezer and adjusts the temperature. After she's eaten her dinner, she takes the food on the table to Brenda's. She knows that Brenda will still be up; it's 10:30. Then Anna drives back home and takes her bath, puts on her pink nightgown, calls Kyle real quick to say good night and goes to sleep.

While she sleeps she has some weird dreams, and some sweet dreams. The weird dreams are about a young lioness that that leaves the pride to live with the sheep. Two lionesses follow her and attack her. The lionesses know she can't beat the both of them, but she makes a valiant effort to hold her own, knowing she's going to lose. A black sheep and a white sheep break off from the flock and come to her aid. The white sheep gets there first and makes its presence known. Then the black sheep comes running as fast as it can and kicks one of the two lionesses in the head without hesitation and staggers that lioness. More shocked than angry, she claws the black sheep once in the face. The white sheep attempts to talk to them, and the two lionesses look at the white sheep, then they look at the three of them, and decide to leave instead of killing the three of them. Then she has a second dream about the brave young lioness, traveling through the woods one dark night to get a drink of that fresh water straight from the river.

When she finishes drinking, she notices a pack of wolves

staring and growling at her while moving in attack formation. It startles her at first as she also noticed that she is bigger and stronger than anyone of them. They surround the lioness, reminding her that she's alone, which frightens her terribly. They attack her. By the end of the fight two wolves are dead, three badly injured, and the other three didn't bother fighting her after that. They run back into the woods, but there is one problem: she also has to go back through the woods, the same direction that the wolves had run in order to get back to the flock. So that's what she does, while of course praying that they didn't attack her again. She has mild injuries, but is very afraid. Lucky for her, they are more afraid. They run from her. One of them keeps on running. The lioness is almost out of the woods when a half man, half horse appeared to the aid of the wolves, armed with a heavy cavalry saber, and a Hunnic bow. He looks strong and barbaric. The wolves are not afraid. It looks as if they are running to him to tell what happened to them and who done it.

This freaks the lioness out. The lioness takes off and runs

out of the woods, through the jungle, across the field, and back to the flock at top speed without looking back.

Anna wakes up in cold sweats and feeling frightened herself. She gets up and goes to the kitchen to eat a pint out of the freezer.

"First two weird dreams in one, then blood for breakfast. My life sucks."

After her breakfast she looks at the clock: 5:51 am. She has slept all night, but she figures she'll just hang out with her loved ones during the day. Then she goes back to bed for a couple more hours of shuteye.

The next dream was about Kyle. She dreams that Kyle has come to her door with a rose one beautiful summer morning and given her a warm hug and kiss, then asked her to come to the beach with him. She happily agreed and got her bikini & sports bra, and headed out with him. He is wearing some tan shorts and a white muscle suit. He has two blankets, volleyball and a Frisbee in the back seat of his truck, and two surfboards on the top of the hood.

They first stop at White Castle to pick up some

burgers, hot fries, some drinks, and a couple of milk shakes. They go to the beach and get with another couple and play a little volleyball. After that, they put one blanket on the sand and cover up with the other.

"Baby how are we going to tan under the blanket?"

"Girl we can make our own heat."

Then they start making love right there on the beach. Then he looks at her and says. "Ah, baby you have to wake up."

"Huh? What?"

"Baby you have to wake up."

The dream fades and she sees black, as her eyes are closed. She'd had a sweet dream indeed as she smiles and stretches her arms and legs. After that, she hears a man's voice.

"Is it waking up? Hurry up."

Unsure if she's still dreaming, she opens her eyes and screams.

"Oh shit she's up!"

She sees a man standing over her with a sharp piece of wood and a big hammer. He tries to stab her, but she grabs his hand and scratches his face, rolls over, gets up and stands on the foot of her bed to run into a second man who is trying to grab her. There's a flash of pink satin as she kicks him in the chest and he falls against the wall. She is knocking them away as she screams, "Please don't hurt me! I will give you money, or whatever you want!"

"Hey guys are you sure that she's one of them?"

Wait a damn minute! Two men and a woman, it's three of them! The first guy tries to stab her again, but she grabs his hand again and pushes him against the woman, and she screams again. "Leave me alone!" The second guy tries to grab her, but she swings an over the head left, and catches him.

Anna goes for her dresser to get her gun. The woman shoots at her with a crossbow, missing Anna's head by only two inches, but that's only because Anna has ducked. Anna once again goes for her dresser and grabs her gun. The first guy rushes at her to try to take the gun, and she screams again, "Somebody help me!" Then she swiftly knees him in the jewels and throws him out of the bedroom window. The second guy is just now getting up, and he's holding his eye. Anna is more concerned about the lady with the crossbow, who has just reloaded and is about to shoot at her again. At the same time, Anna points the pistol at her and they both take their shots.

Anna is hit in the upper part of her stomach. The other woman has caught it in the shoulder, and one has grazed her face as she fell. The guy runs out of the bedroom like a cat. Anna shoots him and the man jumps up like a deer with both hands on his buttocks, trips over her entertainment unit, and knocks the TV over. He falls behind it with both legs up in the air. One of his shoes comes off his foot and flies the other direction as he tumbles forward.

Anna turns her attention to the guy in the back yard. He struggles to get to his feet and hop away, but Anna is watching him, and too angry to feel the burn of the sun. "Hey! Hey! Where you going?" She yells. She shoots him in the back as he tries to run.

Stepping away from the window, out of the sun, Anna walks

over to the woman. The woman drops to her knees and begs

for mercy, but Anna is trying not to hear her. "Girl, get up

and die with some dignity."

"Please don't kill me. I will do anything. You don't have to

shoot me."

This is turning Anna on. For the first time she finds a woman

sexually attractive, and she doesn't know if she wants to kiss

her, bite her, or kill her. She starts to kiss her until she sees

the arrow, still in her stomach. That angers Anna all over

again. She breaks the arrow and pulls it out, then places her

hands around the lady's neck, picks her up off the ground,

and throws her into the bedroom wall. Oh yes, I mean into

the bedroom wall: she is halfway into the bathroom. Anna is

tempted to feed on her right then. She wraps her fingers

around the lady's forearm and pulls it up to her mouth.

Anna's tongue darts out and licks some of the fresh warm

blood off of it. The taste, the sensation the warmth that

spreads through her body has an intoxicating grip on her.

She can barely resist, and she wants more. Anna also feels

the strength she never had, and the strength that she could have. Her senses are sharper than she's ever felt in her life. At the same time, the sun coming in through the window gets a little bit hotter and a whole lot brighter. Anna notices an offensive odor coming from the wall. The woman is wearing a garlic necklace. She had no idea that garlic could smell so terrible, and fights the urge to retch. It makes Anna realized that if she bites this woman, she will never be human again. It would be her first kill as a vampire, even if she just took a little, is a bite a bite? Would she able to control herself to stop? Either way, that smelly necklace has got to go. She pulls it off of her neck and throws it out the window. Then Anna hears sirens, so she pulls the lady out of the wall.

"What is your name?"

The lady is just coming to and barely conscious.

"Where am I? Who are you?"

"What! News flash, my name is Anna Davis, you and your two goons broke into my house and attacked me. Hold on a minute."

It has just occurred to Anna to check on the guy that she shot in the buttocks. He is gone. He left Anna's door wide open, and one of his shoes is still there in the middle of her dining room floor. The TV is busted on the floor behind the shattered glass from her entertainment unit. She shakes her head and takes a deep breath before going back to interrogate the other lady some more. Anna figures that she's given the lady enough time to collect her thoughts and senses.

"Alright, we are going to try this again. What is your name? Do you know me? And why did you attack me?"

"Officer Davis?" A man yells, "Officer Davis are you here? Are you okay?"

"Yeah! I'm back here!"

Then Anna looked at the lady and whispered.

"You're lucky, but I'm still going to find out who you are."

Anna goes through the woman's pockets, trying to find an ID, credit cards, or anything with her name and picture on it.

No luck, just a wallet with four hundred dollars in cash, and a note with addresses in it. One of those addresses is Anna's.

"Girl what the fuck! I should kill you right now!" Anna leans over towards the second drawer of her dresser, drops the wallet in and knees it shut.

"Officer Davis there you are. Are you okay? Who is that?"

"This woman and two other guys broke into my house and attacked me."

"Alright Officer Davis we got it. We are going to need to get her to the hospital right away."

"Can you guys find out her name for me? Also the man in the back yard?"

The officer looks out of the bedroom window.

"Well I'll tell you what, he won't be back. We are going to need two ambulances."

One of the policemen calls for two ambulances. When he sees Anna's shirt, he says they'll need a third.

"No! Not me, I'm fine."

"Look at your shirt."

The woman is barely coherent, and tells the police that the reason that Officer Davis is okay is because she's a vampire. Anna looks at her fellow officers with her eyebrows raised and rolls her eyes. The officers laugh and handcuff the woman, and make fun of her until her ambulance comes.

The ambulances have come and gone. Anna called a service to board up her bedroom window, and the bathroom window the attackers had forced to get in. The men are waiting for the police to clear the scene. One of the officers is on the sidewalk drinking coffee with them, letting them know how much the NYPD appreciates their patience. Anna is sitting at the kitchen table, giving her statement to Officer Brownson, who has what used to be Anna's chair. He's next to the window where, in the late morning, the sun would come in. The blinds and curtains are closed, but Anna feels like she doesn't want to have her back to the sun. While she's talking, it crosses her mind that it would be nice if all the windows were boarded up and she could be safe from these killers, and never have to worry about a stray sunbeam.

When she finally has the house to herself, Anna calls the hospital, looking for Doctor Page. He's not on duty, so she looks through her dresser until she finds his home number and calls him.

A female voice answers, "Hello this is the Page residence." This must be his wife, but to get nervous and hang up now will just create suspicion. "Hello, my name is Anna Davis and I'm looking for Doctor Page."

"Sure, hold on a second." Another woman comes on the line.

"Hello this is Mrs. Page."

Oh boy, Anna thinks. Here goes.

"Hi Mrs. Page. My name is Anna Davis. Sorry I'm calling so early but can I talk to your husband for a moment? It's really important."

"Sure, hold on."

"Hello this is Doctor Page speaking."

"Hello doctor, this is Anna Davis."

"Anna, how are you doing?"

"I got attacked this morning, two men and a woman."

"What?"

"One of the men tried to stab me with a sharp wooden stake, and the lady shot me in the stomach with a crossbow."

Then Mrs. Page chimes in from the extension.

"She's got hunters after her, Aaron."

"Honey why are you listening in on our conversation?"

"Sorry, I just wanted to make sure everything was okay."

"Yeah, okay."

"I'm getting off the phone."

"No wait. I would like you to meet Anna. She is a client of mine, and our newest member."

"Anna, this a my wife Stephanie, and Stephanie, this is Anna."

"Hello Anna."

"Hello Mrs. Page."

"Tell us what happened. My wife is good people. She can help too."

"Okay, I shot one in the butt, and the other dead. The lady I shot in the shoulder and grazed her face. I'm glad that someone called the police for me. She's in the hospital right now. When she gets out the hospital she's going straight to jail. I just want to get her and the other guy's name too."

"Honey if she's at the hospital…"

"Yeah Anna we'll take care of it. So we are looking for a lady with a bullet wound to the shoulder and a graze wound to the face, also, a man who has been shot in the ass, right?"

"Right."

"Can you describe them a little bit more so we don't make any mistakes?"

"Two white males, blondes, and a brunette female. All three of them were wearing blue jeans and black sweaters. I remember the woman was wearing a garlic necklace."

"Got it. We'll get them."

"Thank you. Don't forget to give me their names."

"Their names? Um, sure. Anna do you need me to send a couple of guys to protect you? It's 11:15 and you know it's not safe for you to sleep right now."

His wife chimes in again.

"But Aaron honey, what about us? We have to be careful too, those hunters are as sharp as they are underhanded."

"It's okay, I'm a police officer. That reminds me to call the station and have them watch my house, and a couple people to stay with me. If that's not enough protection, I'm in trouble."

"Wait a minute, you're a cop?"

Anna hears a phone hang up. "Stephanie? Stephanie! Hold on a second Anna, my wife hung up the phone."

Anna waits a good fifteen seconds before they're back on the phone. Stephanie apologizes for being rude. She also explains that she's had distrust for police ever since the Nelson family got exposed. One of the police officers who those people were paying to protect them, turned out to be a hunter. Hunters are humans with the knowledge that vampires exist. They hate vampires, and once one finds out, news spread quickly to other hunters. They are like a pack of wolves.

"What happened to the Nelsons? They all were killed

in their sleep. That police officer was the only hunter that was caught and killed. The others got away."

"Well it looks like I chose the wrong time to get bit."

"Just stay awake for the whole day, and call people who know you, better yet, people who you can trust for protection, if you're going to sleep today."

"I will do that, thank you Mr. & Mrs. Page."

"Oh, and make no mistake; hunters know where you live now. You are going to have to move before they find out anything else about you."

Anna's next call is to Kyle. She explains to him what has happened to her this morning. They hang up at 11:30 and he shows up by 11:55. He is on duty, but this is a police case. When Kyle comes over, she says, "Thank you. I'm glad that you came; now I can get some sleep."

"What? How can you sleep at a time like this? Are you crazy?"

"No, those hunters are waiting for me to fall asleep so they can break into my place and kill me."

"This sounds like a movie. I don't know how much more of

this… never mind. We'll get through this."

After running out to his truck for a moment, Kyle comes in to the bedroom and starts kissing Anna. She kisses him back, and for a quick moment she wonders if he just wants some. Well if so, she figures that she'd better enjoy every moment with him before the day comes that he comes to his senses and runs from her faster than Goldilocks from three serial killers. He bends her over and pulls her nightgown up. She is with it.

It is sudden and brief and passionate. They seem to want to crash into each other, as quickly and violently as possible. Afterwards, Kyle is lying diagonally across half the bed, weak and clasping Anna. At this point, she was no longer able to control herself.

"Baby I love you."

She bites him lightly, then whispers in his ear.

"Baby you are mine forever, forever and ever."

In that split second, Kyle knows that he is in trouble. Anna tries to bite him, and he's never moved so fast in his life. He ducks away from her and at the same time uses his hand to push Anna's head away from his shoulder and neck area.

Kyle quickly gets to his feet and tries to run, but falls over his own pants, which were still around his ankles.

"Where are you going?"

Her eyes are almost cat-like, and her canine teeth long and sharp. Kyle's eyes grow wide with surprise, and he pulls his pants up and tries to run. Anna grabs the back of his pants and pulls him close. He tries to yank away, but it's useless. He can't believe how strong she is; he can't even offer a decent struggle.

"Anna chill out!"

"Oh sorry. I got a little carried away. Can I have a hug?"

Kyle eyes her suspiciously for a moment while he pulls up his pants and buckles his belt, but he gives her a smile and opens his arms. Anna smiles back at him, puts her arms out and leans into him. As soon as his hands touch Anna's sides, Kyle turns his palms out and shoves her over the couch. When Anna jumps up, she sees him running for the door. She picks up a pillow and throws it at his head. Kyle has the door open, but that flying pillow to the head is what made him stagger through it. He hits the bar on the outside door clutches it with on hand, finding his balance on the stoop.

"Kyle I hate you! You're an asshole!"

It's 12:15 in the afternoon, and there are a whole lot of people out walking, driving, and standing around. The sun is high, and the entrance to the building is shaded. More and more people stop what they're doing to look and laugh at the guy getting charged up by his chick. Kyle decides that the two of them are drawing too much attention for Anna's safety.

"Baby chill for a minute, I have to talk to you."

"Don't you 'baby' me! Chill my ass! And that was real cold!"

"I'm not trying to be cold, just calm down and listen for a minute."

"You calm down! And I'm not listening to shit! Get the hell

out my house!"

"I am out of your house!"

They have an audience now. At least twenty people are gathered around, many laughing so hard they can barely stay on their feet without leaning on something. Anna notices she's losing control of herself and causing and scene. So she calms down and motioned him back in. Kyle on the other hand was hesitant about that idea.

"Come in I'm not going to do anything."

A lady from the crowd said, "Yeah girl, but don't let him off too easy. From now on he'd better be a good boy."

Anna is thankful for that clueless woman's comment; it means that she doesn't have to think of a lie to tell the noisy and entertained crowd, who are already discussing the two of them like they were a reality TV show.

Kyle follows Anna inside, and to the kitchen. She takes out a couple of pint bags and eats right in front of Kyle.

"I said I'm not going to hurt you. Why you look so nervous?"

"You tried to bite me."

"I'm sorry, I got carried away, but I wasn't going to kill you. That I know for a fact. My cravings were only to taste you."

"Do you have to eat that stuff right in front of me like that?"

"Oh no. I would have turned you into a vampire. I'm evil Kyle."

  Then she turns on the water works and Kyle melts like ice cream. Anna runs off to her room for a moment, and comes back to the living room and falls asleep on his lap for an hour. She wakes up to the phone ringing. A desk sergeant at the precinct is calling to inform her that Olivia Bloom, the woman at the hospital, has escaped. "How did you let her escape?" Anna yells. "Her name needs to be Olivia Houdini."

"I understand Ms. Davis, the hospital informed us just a minute ago. We are going to protect you. We'll watch over you and your place 24/7, and even help you relocate if you choose to, which in your case, would be a good idea."

"Thank you. I'm going to need all the help I can get."

"No problem, tell Kyle over there that the captain wants to talk to him."

Anna almost choked.

"Okay hold on." She gives the phone to Kyle, and gets close so she can listen.

"Hello."

"Detective Miller, how are things coming along with your investigation?"

"Going just fine Sir. Anna got attacked this morning and the police got the last attacker in custody at the hospital."

"Okay then detective, I see you're on top of things huh?"

"Yes sir."

"I figured that, but it's not this case. The hospital just called and informed us that the lady escaped the hospital. Her name is Olivia Bloom. Since you're already assigned to this case, I'm leaving you in charge of finding Olivia and bringing her straight here into custody. She will not give us the slip again."

"Yes sir. I hear you sir."

When Kyle hangs up, Anna is laughing.

"What's so funny?"

"You guys. The two of you sound like the cartoon Inspector Gadget. I got to call Doctor Page."

Anna calls Doctor Page, but Mrs. Page answers again.

"Hi Anna. You're calling about what we told the police?"

"Yeah, how did you know?"

"Because we took care of it."

"Huh?"

"We took care of both of them. You know what I mean.
Those are two that you won't have to worry about again.
Well, my husband is asleep and I'm in the middle of selling a
condo right now."

"Selling a house?"

"Yes, I'm a real-estate agent. The only reason why I'm up
during the day."

"That's pretty impressive. Okay, well, thanks and good luck.
I'll talk to you later I guess."

"Sure, after five but before 7 pm."

Anna knows that Kyle was put in charge of finding Olivia,
what will she tell him? What should she tell him? Anna has
never lied to Kyle, intentionally, and doesn't plan to start
now.

"Baby what was that about?"

"Um, um, shit. That was my doctor's wife. She basically said… how do I put this?"

"Just tell me the truth."

"She basically told me that I don't have anything to worry about."

"Because they took care of it for you?"

"How did you know? You heard us?"

"Yeah, I'm not going to say anything, but did you have to go to the mafia?"

"That wasn't the mafia?"

"Sounds like it. You sure?"

"I'm sure."

"Well who are they?"

She sighs. At least he has enough respect not to try to pick her brain like a closer would. He is straight up.

"They… if I tell you, this too can't leave this room."

"It will stay between me and you, like everything else."

"My doctor and his wife are both vampires."

"They are vampires?"

"Doctor Page saved my life a couple of times. He gave me

two blood transfusions when I didn't know what was going on, or what I have become."

Kyle stays for another hour and goes to the hospital, signs in and asks the doctors, nurses, and the security team a couple of routine questions. He gets their names, and leaves the hospital for the police station, and writes up their statements. The time is 3:53pm. After that he goes out to eat.

7

Anna calls Brenda.

"Hi Anna, what's up girl?"

"Nothing at all girl. Well I'm lying. I need you to come watch my back."

"What's going on? Those vampires after you again? Do I need to bring my heat?"

"No it's not vampires this time."

"Oh good."

"It's vampire hunters. So you might want to bring that heat, just in case."

"I'm on the way."

"Thank you. Listen, I just need to sleep in the day."

"Alright, I'm on the way."

Twenty minutes later, Brenda comes over. Anna explains to

her what happened, then shows her around. "Damn Girl. Looks like somebody had done a little demolition work in the bedroom."

"Yeah, I had to throw that woman into the wall."

"There is a little blood over there. Did you clean up most of it? Well, there's still arrows and bullet holes all over the place. Can I call my other home girl? Because I don't want to be here by myself either. You know, while you're asleep."

"Sure go ahead. As a matter of fact, I'm going to order pizza and wings, so bring whoever you like."

Brenda calls her girlfriend Julian and informs her that she has to hold Anna down for the day and that she might want to bring her gun. Then she asks Julian if she could bring some weed and tells her that Anna was buying pizza and wings. Julian wants to know who they're going to be protecting Anna from. Brenda explains that two men and a woman attacked Anna and that she'll need their protection for the day, and gives Julian the address. Julian arrives a half hour later. She's slightly taller than the both of them, and skinny, a pretty dark skinned lady with short hair in finger waves and pretty brown eyes. Seventeen years old, she was Brenda's young, impressionable friend, student, and solider. Most of what she knows about the side of the law, from boosting to small time hustling, she learned from Brenda.

"Hi Brenda."

"Hi Julian, I'm glad you could make it. Oh, Julian this is Anna, Anna this is Julian."

"Hi, you must be Ms. Davis. I have seen you around sometimes."

"Really? I think I remember you."

"Yeah well, I definitely remember you. You arrested me once."

"Oh yeah wow, it's a small world. You know I gave you a huge break right? I only took you in for the boosting, and took the drugs from you, I even let you keep the money."

"And I appreciate that Ms. Davis. You told me to get my act together."

"I like those shoes Julian. Are they Prada?"

"Yes they are. Thank you I'm glad you like them."

"How much did you pay for them?"

"Come on Ms. Davis, understand that I'm risking my life over here right now to hold you down."

"It's cool I'm not a robot, and from now on I consider you a close friend."

"Yeah Julian, Anna is cool. Hey did you bring the weed?"

"Yes. I brought four nicks."

"Did you bring your gun?"

Now Julian is kind of nervous standing right in front of a cop, who had already arrested her once. Brenda notices that, pulls out her handgun, and lays it on the living room table.

"See, I got mine. You good, trust me."

"Yeah you good Julian, I already knows you came strapped when my girl Brenda called you. I like you leather jacket. You are jazzy indeed, and I don't hate."

Julian starts laughing. She realizes that, not only does Anna know that she's strapped, but she knows that everything Julian has on is fly and at the top of the line, and stolen. She has on one of the nicest black leather coats she's laid eyes on, a top of the line pair of blue jeans and black hood sweat shirt, all parade.

"Thank you. Okay, I brought my strap right here." Julian pulls out a 1911 .45 cal from her hip, made by Smith & Weston, and laid it on the table.

"Damn! Girl you're not playing. Even Brenda's pistol is bigger than mine. I only have a 9 mm."

"Yeah, I figured that if we're headed for a gunfight, my little ass better bring a big one. This will turn them away or blow them away."

"Wow, how old are you?"

"Seventeen. But I had a good teacher."

"Brenda? You're a bad influence. Wait a minute, if you're the teacher, why aren't you getting it like Julian?"

"Anna you know why. Because you rode me like a horse. I think you busted me 6 or seven times, and gave me the 'I know you, don't even think about it' look all the other times. So I had to slow the boosting down, way down, and had to stop hustling completely. You almost didn't let me buy my own smoke."

"Ha ha ha oh yeah, that's right."

"Wow. I didn't know Sister Davis had radar on you like that."

"Yeah girl, it was terrible. Remember I told you about it? That's why I didn't want you shopping with me; you would've been on her radar too."

"Yeah I wouldn't let Brenda get away with anything once I noticed her. Not for a while. Eventuality we became good friends."

"Yeah I remember you told me. Ms. Davis, you are a hot mess. I wouldn't think in an million years that you would have Brenda stick up that lady."

"What lady?"

"That lady who was trying to take your detective friend to the cleaners at court."

"Oh shit."

"Yeah, you didn't think I knew about that. That was off the chain funny. I never leaked it."

The pizza and wings arrive. Brenda pays the man and tips him, and carries the food above her shoulder like a waitress as she walks over to the coffee table.

"Hey y'all I got the pizza and wings, let's eat."

"Ya'll go ahead and eat. I already have a little food left and I will eat in my room."

"Huh? But don't you want eat with... Oh that's right."

"Brenda what is wrong with Ms. Davis? Ms. Davis are you ok?"

"Well she's um, she's um, Anna can I tell her?"

"What! No! Are you trying to get me killed or something?"

"But Ms. Davis, Brenda and I are here for you, and you know our secrets. Besides, secrets keep you sick; especially hiding them from... you know what, my bad I'm tripping. I'm sure you have a good reason."

"Well people already know anyway. You ready for this one?"

"Yeah go ahead."

"I'm a vampire, and people are trying to kill me."

Julian just laughs. "You're a riot! Brenda why aren't you laughing? I thought she was pretty funny. Anna is that a bag of blood you're holding? That's gross"

"Yeah Julian, I was bitten a little over a week ago by a man, after I chased a lady through an alley."

"That was you? Brenda why didn't you tell me?"

"Oh me? I was too busy getting shot at, kidnapped, and beat down, while helping Anna fight off suck head bitches."

"Hey!"

"Sorry Anna, no offence."

"None taken."

"Well I still don't believe it."

Anna grabs Julian by the front of her leather coat with one hand and lifts her straight to the ceiling. Julian is scared and nearly pulls her gun on Anna.

"Girl calm down. You know I'm not going to hurt you."

"Oh my God you're strong!"

"See? But I didn't have super strength like this before last week, and the sun will burn me. Now do you believe me?"

"Yes. That is for sure."

"Well, I will let you guys eat, and I will eat my food."

"Okay Anna. You know Julian and I will be up on the front."

Julian stops her with a question. "Wait Ms. Davis? How did all this stuff start?"

"Brenda?" Why don't you do the honors?"

Brenda laughs because Anna knows that she's dying to tell it. While Anna eats in the kitchen, Brenda explains everything that happened over the past eight days over pizza and wings. She's barely even started the story when she remembers that they don't have drinks, and goes to the kitchen to get Julian and herself some lemonade.

"Brenda, I'm eating in here."

"Girl I already know you. You're all right."

When Anna has finished eating, she had a serious talk with Brenda. "Hey girl, I'm getting tired and it's 5:30, I need to sleep."

"Okay, well get some sleep. I know what time it is."

"Listen, I'm really scared. People are trying to kill me while I'm asleep, and they will if you leave me. So, please don't leave me."

"I'm not going to leave you. Here, we will make up the couch for you."

Before they could get started, the phone rings.

"Anna is that you?"

"Yes. Who's calling?"

"This is Detective Robinson and my partner, Detective Walker. Are you okay in there?"

"Yes, thank you. Where are you guys?"

"Come on, you know the answer to that. We're watching over your home."

"Thank you. I will need all the help I can get."

"No problem. Tell your two hoodlum girl friends we said 'hi.'"

"Really?"

"Well no don't do that. Just know that they might not know us, but they have our utmost respect from now on. We have some undercover watching the back. So far, no other funny stuff has been going on since this morning."

"Thank you. I needed to hear that."

"No problem, bye."

Brenda and Julian have overheard half of the conversation, so they don't bother asking who it was. They just get to work fixing up the couch for Anna to sleep on. The girls watch over her like guardian Angels.

The Brass Hand Do-jan in Pawtucket, Rhode Island is an imposing structure: a low slung brick industrial building with glass-block windows on a side street that dead ends at the railroad tracks. Tommy Kerr, its owner, is equally imposing, despite his small stature. Barely 5'6", he has a tight, muscular body and a sense of confidence in it that makes people understand that he is a serious person. When he inclines himself forward, and bores his brown eyes under close-cropped black hair at someone, they listen.

That is the reaction his students are having as he finishes up his last class for the day. Like most of his classes, this one is full at 20 students. "Alright so remember, if you can avoid a fight, its better. You can actually talk your way out of 90 percent of any fight. However, if you must, or choose to accept a challenge, keep in mind four things. Number one: know that it is on and you have done your best to avoid it. Number two: it is okay to be afraid. If you can admit this, than you are much less of a coward than the man who doesn't. So hurry up and kick his ass and get it done. Which brings us to number three: stay in control of yourself. Don't strike in anger or your moves will be slow and sloppy. You won't even hit hard. Last but not least, when you hit, stay mindful of your form and strike proper. The rest will fall into place. Does anyone have any questions?"

"I do."

"Yes Michael. Go ahead."

"Yeah this guy tried to kick my ass because he thought I was eyeing his girl. He thought he could pound on me because he was big and muscular, and I'm kind of skinny."

"Ok, what happened?"

"I gave him a two-piece like you taught me, one swift jab and a stiff straight, from the ground, to my legs, to my shoulder. He fell and he tried to get back up. I was scared out of my mind, so I stomped him in the mouth and got back in my car. He was still out when I drove away. His girl friend was screaming that I killed him. This frightened me even more. So I turned the corner and put the pedal to the metal. Was that wrong?" The whole class laughed, and then got silent.

"Absolutely not. It's always better not to get caught. Oh, I heard something about that, it happened two days ago. No he is not dead he just got a good ass-whipping, and the next time he might not be so eager to show off for his little girl friend. Alright class dismissed. Oh and by the way, please don't kill anybody. You guys know what you're learning. The last thing we need is police and the News pointing fingers at the Brass Hand. Ok dismiss."

While his class put back on their street clothes and went home, Tommy went to answer the phone in the office between the large and small training rooms. He used to get most of his fighting experience in the street, until his dad put him in the golden gloves boxing tournaments at age 16, against his mother's wishes. Although his father tried talking to him, he would still get into fights at school. Most of the time he would lose. His father tried whooping him. This made him whoop on kids that provoked him. So his father put him in the golden gloves. He couldn't stop him from fighting, so he might as well do it for sportsmanship. Some day he could get paid for it. Tommy boxed for two years, until one day he came home from a match looking like he'd got hit by a truck. His mother almost was in tears. She beat her husband up and made him take him out of boxing.

So they decided together to put him in Tae Kwon Do. His mom and dad would go watch some of his classes. His mom even showed up to the fight tournaments, which surprised the hell out of the father. He stayed for three years and left a second degree black belt. He also had a job at the local gas station and had plans on going to college that year. He was 21 and his life was starting to look pretty good, when his dad was killed one night in a mysterious way. The police said that someone had stabbed him in the neck twice. He and his mom took it pretty hard. Who would want t kill his dad? He was an honest man and didn't have any enemies. After they buried him, a month later, they were faced with harsh reality: the bills. Rent, lights, gas and the fact that they refused to bury him indecently. They used her credit card to pay for the burial. Tommy and his mother were up crap's creek without a paddle in debt.

A couple days later, a strange man had knocked on their door. He said his name was Steven Evans and he didn't usually make personal visits, but he would like to talk to him alone if it was okay. Tommy agreed to speak to him. Steven said that he found out that Tommy was a great fighter, a black belt even, and seemed like a good guy. He offered him an underground gig, pit fighting. It turns out Steven knew some people who ran these fights, and there were huge amounts of money going down on them. Tommy would fight once a week, and be paid $1500 a fight to start. But Steven warned him not to end the fight too quickly, nor to beat the opponents too badly. They have to appear to have a good chance against him, since he was a new fighter in the underground.

Tommy agreed head first and fought once a week, and won the purse each time. He made easy money for four months beating up on chumps. Steven felt that it was time to step up to the real fighters, the martial artists. Tommy was kind of nervous but he was with it. His first fight with the big leagues was a brown belt in Tae Kwon do. He beat him and won $3000, and paid off a few very lucky gamblers who took him at 17-1.

After that, Steven had him fighting other black belts. Tommy took them on them one by one and by the end of his sixth month as a pit fighter, he had over $50,000 banked. But fighting black belts were brutal. He had to slow down, to one fight every two weeks. Tommy only lost one fight, and that was against a man named Johnny Lee. The following month, a fighter from the Southern European circuit showed up, fighting under the name Bad Karma. Tommy told Steven flat out that he could not beat Bad Karma, and that he would get his ass whooped, and possibly put in the hospital. Steven believed him 100 percent and understood, so he lied and said that Tommy was in a car accident and was in the hospital. If it had been true, he might have shared a room with Johnny Lee, as soon as Bad Karma had finished with him. Steven knew that they had both did what was in their best interest, even though it was kind of punkish. Steven had saved Tommy's face, his rep, and his ass.

Steven got Tommy a second gig as one of his personal bodyguards, and every once in a while, a drug lord robber. See, Steven's Uncle was a Major in the State Police

Narcotics Task Force, and the liaison to the DEA. One of his cousins was a detective. What Steven would do sometimes for a larger amount of quick cash is talk to his uncle and his cousin, and they would give him intelligence about who was on the verge of getting busted. Steven would get his uncle and his cousin together with a couple of Steven's own guys and raid the big time drug dealer. They only did it that big a couple of times, and it was always out of their jurisdiction. But to drug lords, cops are cops. You do what they say now, and ask questions later. It was a quick hundred grand, at least, and a couple of kilos and guns every time. The third and last time was in Denver. They took a private plane to Denver. They had police vests but had to buy some of the guns at a local store. They raided the biggest drug lords in Denver. They took them for $250,000 and six kilos and left some small change for the Denver PD. Steven's cousin expressed doubts about the operation. The Denver police had their hearts set on a surplus Abrams tank from Iraq. "Those assholes have enough toys, and you don't even have an X-box," one of Steven's guys yelled at him.

During these times Tommy had saved Steven's life twice, and shown Steven that he had a good head on his shoulders, so Steven made him his right hand man. Steven finally told Tommy what had happened to his dad. He told him that Mr. Kerr was bitten in the neck and killed by a vampire. Tommy naturally did not believe him. So he took him to meet two couples who were vampires. The four of them lived in one big mansion, the Walstons and the Petersons. They were the only vampires protected by the hunters, which to Steven didn't make any sense. He explained to Tommy that those four were somehow in the good graces of the vampire hunters. The first in command, the boss, was protecting them. Apparently the story goes that these four vampires got in deep trouble with the vampire council over in Europe, for all kinds of charges like, helping humans, befriending humans, attacking their own kind to defend humans, trying to get other vampires to eat pint bags instead of killing people. The worst one was exposing their existence to their families and close friends without permission of their council.

The council had ordered both their friends and families, to be slaughtered. But one of their vampire friends had given them the heads up. Now their friends and families are anywhere except Europe. Now the Petersons and Walstons own some low-end commercial properties and a couple of Laundromats, and they have a couple of their family members living with them. The council wouldn't dare step foot on Rhode Island. They know better.

Tommy could not believe how strong they were, plus they were very smart, polite, and friendly, which would make you forget that they are vampires, and could kill you quickly. Good thing they were good. The fact that they couldn't go out in the sun had to suck.

On the drive home, Tommy worked up the courage to ask Steven's opinion on something. He wanted to open his own martial arts school. Steven thought that it was a brilliant idea, but first Tommy would have to fight a couple of more fights, not just for the money, but also for the rep. Six months is a long time in the underground. When Tommy came back to the pit fights, the people who remembered him looked at him as if they had seen a ghost. Then they cheered. Tommy was back. Thank goodness that Bad Karma was back in Spain. The betting money was unconvinced, which was all the better for the people who believed in him. After Tommy won the fight, Steven told the announcer to blow up his name and the fact that he was about to open up a martial arts school in Pawtucket. Steven also called his wife, and had her find a building and help decorate it. She did, and she did a fine job too. Steven wasn't a good decorator. Leave it to him and he would have made it look like a gun store. Tommy had his school up and ready before too long. He figured that he would need some help so he hired his friend Jerry from Tae know do, another black belt. Jerry understood that Tommy was trying to get on his feet, so he didn't take a lot of his money. If he knew about the money that he was making, he probably would have, but he didn't. Besides, it was only three hours a day. When the place was done, business was slow for almost a month. The classes were half-full, if that. Jerry was only 23, the same age as

Tommy at the time, and Tommy knew that Jerry would quit on him, as soon as Tommy got half way on his feet if he didn't pay Jerry right. So he paid him. Although Tommy was paying him out of his pocket every day, he thought it was worth it. He paid Jerry $1500 for the month. His rent was only $2000 a month, thanks to a deal Steven's wife had got for him. Jerry also had offered him $700 back. But Tommy said to hold on to it for him. The fourth week fifty people wanted to sign up for classes. Wow, was that a blessing for them. Tommy wanted to train the first class of 20 people on Mondays, Wednesdays, and Saturdays. He had 40 people on the books, paying 250 a month, and to his surprise, they said it was a decent deal and paid it with no problem.

That is what Tommy has been doing for the last five years now, teaching. So many of his students have left his class as black belts, trained by Tommy Kerr and Jerry Clerk. The class almost always stayed full because everybody knew that any one of his students will whip your butt. He also has some of his students in the underground pit fights, and when they hit you, you fall. His white belts are good, and they hit pretty hard. So an orange belt was that much better. You didn't want to fight a green belt. You would hate to fight a brown belt. So his black belts you would probably run away from. Sometimes the story would go like this.

"So you want to fight huh? Who trained you chump?"

"Tommy Kerr."

"Oh, okay. Wait a minute who? You know I don't have any problems with you right?"

The class is over, and everyone is on their way home except Michael, who is talking to Jerry. Tommy reaches the phone in the office.

"Brass hand do'."

"Hey Tommy, this is Steven. I sent three of my people to a suck-head's house down in Manhattan on some cat burglar Ninja shit. The problem is, that one is dead, and the other two are missing. Now I know that Olivia was escorted to the hospital by the NYPD. It's even in the paper. Something went wrong. Something is still wrong. I know Olivia, she would have called by now."

"Maybe she's still at the hospital and didn't get a chance to call yet."

"No, she's not in the hospital. I called and they told me she left to escape the police."

"So she's laying low?"

"Maybe so. But it doesn't make sense that nobody has heard from Olivia or Mark, and Allen is dead. Olivia was shot in the shoulder and the face, and Mark was shot in the ass, and the both of them left the hospital the same day?"

"Yeah, that doesn't add up."

"The worst part about it is that I heard that this suck-head is a cop. I'm worried Tommy. I think the police took my guys, killed them and threw them in the river. Hell if they are good cops, they just have them locked up somewhere. Either way this is not good; the wrong people could get a hold of them. I need you to go down there and find out what happened. Right now I'm about ready to buy that RPG I've had my eye on and pay this Anna girl and her station a little visit!"

"No don't do that. I'll go down there and find out what's going on."

Tommy got Anna's address and a description, and then promised to go down there first thing tomorrow morning.

Tommy put his head on his hand and exhaled. Steven was really pissed, and when Steven was really pissed, and when Steven said that he would buy an RPG and blow up the Manhattan police station, and then Anna, in whichever order he said, he would probably do it. Well he most certainly would blow up her house without a doubt. He was usually a calm, cool and collected person, but if he had a problem with you, then you were in trouble. Oh, and his men were not afraid to make places look like an action movie scene.

Steven's Mother and his sister were killed by a group of vampires called the Nelson family. Steven was 15 years old at the time. Steven's mom tried to make him go over to her friend's birthday party with her. Fortunately, he didn't feel like going. His mom and sister went without him, and never came back. He told his father, who told his brother, who was a cop at the time.

The uncle knew that the Nelsons were vampires, and

that they had to have killed them. There was even a cop and a couple other people protecting and running errands for them. Steven's uncle warned them to stay away from the Nelsons because they were vampires, and they sometimes kill people. They didn't listen and Steven's mom and sister wound up disappearing. Steven, his father Carl, and Steven's uncle Dion broke into the house in the day time and killed them all in their sleep. The bodies of the Nelsons disappeared to dust and they found the bodies of Carl Evans' wife and daughter in the basement, with what looked like stab wounds to the neck, and drained of blood. There was a vampire who was a neighbor of the Nelsons. He made a couple of phone calls, and got together a small group of his humans, followers, pets, whatever, and killed Carl right in front of his son. Carl had just come back from work. He parked his car in front of the house and got out. He still had on his car mechanics uniform with his name in cursive on the left side of his chest. The time was 6:00pm, and the sky was dark, cloudy, and about to rain. Steven heard a commotion and looked out the window and saw his father getting attacked by four people. He opened the front door and screamed.

"Hey get off of my dad!"

Then he heard a voice.

"Get the kid too."

So little Steven ran and got his daddy's gun and shot the first man who ran in the door after him. Then Steven stepped outside. The other three men ran. The only person who was still there was the vampire. He was feeding on his father. Steven shot him in the shoulder. Then the vampire said, "Do you know how bad you just fucked up?"

Steven shot him in the head. He went back inside and grabbed one of the wooden stakes that his father and uncle had made, and came back outside. By this time, everyone on his street had come outside to see what was going on.

As for the vampire, he staggered to his feet and tried to run, but was too injured to get far. Steven shot him in the head again. When he fell, Steven took the wooden stake and put it through his heart. The vampire instantly turned to dust and disintegrated. The whole street had witnessed this in disbelief. They called the police and told them what they saw; the police had a hard time believing them. In fact they didn't believe at all . Dion and his partner were the first cops on the scene. The police arrested the other three guys who took part in killing Carl, but refused to believe a story about a man turning to dust. Dion had Steven stay six blocks over with the Howard family, some people who worked with his father. Dion couldn't let Steven stay with him because he didn't have room, or the constant protection, but the Howards had kind of a big family. Mr. and Mrs. Joe Howard had 4 children; he had 3 boys who were 15, 16 and 17, and one girl who was 14 years of age. Joe Howard had a younger Brother named Edwin Howard and a younger sister named Sallie Howard.

Now Edwin Howard and his wife lived only two houses down. They had three children, two girls, one 17 and one 16, and the boy was 15 years of age. Sallie Howard had a boy friend and she only had two children, she had a 16 and a 14 year old. They lived upstairs from Edwin.

They took Steven in at Dion's request. Dion and Carl

Kerr had known them for years. So Steven was kind of familiar with them, but he had his own friends. It didn't matter though, because it was the Howard family who took him in and treated him like family. The Howards were slick and unlawful people, but what Dion liked about them, was that the parents had imbued in them to always look out for family thick and thin. If you wanted to fight a Howard, you better ask if you can get a one on one. The Howard children were all running some kind of game, drugs or pimping or gambling. Joe and Edwin Howard lied on their job applications eight years before. They didn't know lick about being car mechanics at the time. It was Sallie Howard who got her two brothers those jobs, when the brothers were still back in Queens.

One of Sallie's girl friends was working as a prostitute for one of the pimps. She told Sallie about this guy she was with from up in Rhode Island. He was a real loser and kind of ugly. He would pay her the $300 then he would give her an extra 50 to keep for herself. She put the 50 in her shoe to hide from her pimp. This guy owned a mechanic shop up there. So he had something going for himself. Sallie asked her for the guys name and address. The girl told her with no problem. Then Sallie went to Rhode Island and found him. She played it smooth, not aggressive. Everywhere the guy went she was there in something super sexy. Each time she saw him, she just gave him a smile and said hi, and he spoke back. This went on for a week before she got frustrated and asked him if he wanted to hang out, and he said hell yeah without even thinking.

Before he knew it, she was his hang out buddy, and her two brothers had good jobs, as she planned. Carl hated training those two why would the boss hire two of the dumbest. The Howards knew nothing about fixing cars.

Sallie made sure she didn't let him, nor her brothers know for a year. She started to genially like him by then, and they were kind of friends with benefits. By the second year she told him and he forgave her wholeheartedly. The two brothers were slightly upset at first, but they were much more thankful. So you see, those Howards were something else from the very beginning.

Besides, Steven's aunt and his cousin lived around the corner from them. He also quickly got back in contact with his friends from his old neighborhood. They loved Steven and found that they liked the Howards as well.

The Howards had a hard time believing in such things, until they showed them one.

Now some of Steven's friends were tuff, Steven himself was the tuff and by far the craziest, most violent and daring after all the stuff he went through. But most of Steven's old friends were soft and passive, some even scared. After hanging with the Howards, weren't any of them soft. Eventually they had turned into a gang, and they were gangsters. Later on, Steven's uncle got promoted and he brought in Steven's cousin, then Edwin Howard's youngest daughter, and five of Steven's friends. They still were down and tight and played ridiculous favor just as much. Now one of the Howard daughters is a police Officer, while others liked staying constantly ill-legit.

Steven Evans would become second in command of the

hunters' organization. He was bold, brave and brilliant. He would not order the Howards, they raised him. He would not order around the friends he grow up with, or any of his family, but if he asked them to, they would take care of whatever. It is their intention that you don't hear of them. If you're in the underground you will meet some of them. So make no mistake, it you cross those Rhode Island white boys. You will be sorry.

So Tommy understood why Steven was crazy. The only person crazier and more powerful than him was the boss. Steven had seen how the boss once helped the Petersons and the Walstons get their Mansion and their two laundry mats. It was back in the mid 1980s; the two couples fled Europe and came to America with a few of their family members. They came with nothing except a little bit of money, just enough to pay two months of rent. Lucky for them the boss heard about them and decided to help them. His name is Eric Prochiny. He went to talk to them and they knew that he was a great guy, he was strong and just a little barbaric looking. The four vampires were afraid of him at first. He said that he already knew who they were, and he was going to help them. He said that he was going to help them get some quick money but the mortals with them would have to stay home. Three weeks later on a dark rainy day the clouds were gray and heavy, and it was raining like crazy. The two vampire couples were concerned that they might burn in the sun. Eric assured them that they would not burn as long as the sun did not shine on them. Very few vampires are aware of this; they won't come out in daylight hours at all for any reason. He asked them to keep this a top secret before taking the four of them to Manhattan where they hit two birds with one stone. They robbed a brinks truck, and the bank that it was delivering to, only using make up as mask. With their hair dyed cherry red, and wearing fake tattoos, but using real guns, they went to work fiercely. When the man opened the door and stepped out of the brinks, Eric shot him in the middle of his vest with a .45 caliber and knocked him straight back. The man fell in-between the door. Then he and Jack Peterson rushed inside and hand cuffed all three guards. He gave Jack instructions to bag the money while he and Robert Walston hit up the Bank. He didn't use their names of course. They made the people open the vault and told everybody to go in and get the money. Prochiny told Robert to go in there with them so they don't try any funny stuff and gave him a big duffle bag, while Mrs. Linda Walston held the vault door open.

They got away with $3 million without even one of them getting shot. That robbery made the news big time. Steven even remembers hearing about the first time when he was seven years old. His mom told him, "Hey Steven, these people are getting crazy out here. Today some people robbed the bank and the brinks for an untold amount of cash, and they want them. I feel sorry for those people when they get caught."

Well she was right about one thing; they were wanted for about at least five different felony charges during that robbery. But they had too many of the wrong leads. They were looking for people with tattoos, cherry red hair, and people who looked like other people.

Eric gave them a million and a half dollars. They bought the old mansion and two laundry mats.

Jack and Melissa Peterson, along with Robert and Linda Walston had made a great investment, but burned through the money buying the mansion and these laundry mats. So Eric gave them anther 250 thousand dollars and suggested that they hold on to it for an emergency. But the laundry mats did well, much better than they had expected. They have been doing well ever since. They were afraid to pull off that move back then, but Eric saw no reason why a vampire of all people, would be poor or broke. He was at war with the evil council, and their members. They are extremely rich and powerful. Even their vampire solders were powerful. Also the mortals who served the soldiers were usually middle class, or they were high paid and ill-legit. If they were poor, the vampires might recruit them and put great jobs in their laps. Still, no human was allowed to see or know who a council member was, except a well-trusted and powerful member, some were even government officials of that country. So Eric had no time to fight young and dumb, or weak vampires. He was a vampire slayer.

Tommy wasn't really supposed to know all of this about the first in command. Steven had told him this, and the fact that he introduced him to the Petersons and the Walstons, was enough proof right there. Tommy started to wonder if he was getting in over his head with this chick from Manhattan. Plus she was a police officer, oh boy. To him, tomorrow was going to be like a trip to Mars.

8

Brenda and Julian finally wake Anna up at 11:30.

"Hey girl it's time to get up."

"Huh? Oh. What time is it?"

"The time is 11:30 at night, and Julian has school tomorrow."

Julian nods. "Yeah that's true. But are you going to be all right?"

"I will, thank you. Brenda knows that I should be up by now anyway. Do you need a ride home? Sure you do."

Anna gets up and gives Brenda and Julian a ride home. They drop off Julian first, because she's only 17, and has school tomorrow. Brenda is still concerned for Anna's safety.

"Are you sure you're going to be all right?"

"Oh yeah, I'll be fine. My fellow officers are watching my

apartment 24/7. Besides I'll be up anyway."

"Well okay, but you can stay at my place if you need to for a while. My mom won't mind. You can stay in my room."

"Why thank you, and I will definitely keep that in mind. No I'm just kidding; your mom would kill you. Plus I wouldn't put your family in danger."

Then Brenda goes into her building. Anna goes to the hospital to get some more pint bags of blood from Dr. Page. He gives her another black plastic garbage bag to put the pint bags in, and they both laugh because she forgot to bring a big purse again. Then she heads back to her place.

When she arrives back to her apartment, Carol, James, and Donna are sitting outside on the stairs. All three of them just sitting there, apparently waiting on her to come back home. That's pretty damn bold; can you believe these jerks? Anna parks her car across the street, then gets out and walks toward them, keeping cool not to pull out her 9mm and shot them. "How dare you! Why are y'all in front of my house? What do you want? She yells.

"James she's scared."

"I know Donna."

"Donna you are so blonde, and banned from talking."

"Carol please, not right now. As a matter of fact, both of you ladies better let me do the talking. First of all, we are not here to hurt you."

"I should have ordered my boyfriend to kill you, now it's too late."

"What?"

"Carol no, come on now."

"Sorry, but we don't like her."

"I know, but right now we all have to get along."

"What are the three of y'all stooges talking about?"

Before they could answer Anna's question, a police car pulled up.

It has been sitting three blocks away. Two officers, parked in the middle of the street, right in front of Anna's place. They get out. One officer looks at James, then Carol and Donna. Then the officer looks straight at Anna and asks, "Is everything all right folks?" The cop looks again at Anna.

"Yes officer, everything is okay."

"Okay. We're here to protect and serve."

"Thank you officers, but we're fine."

The cops pull away. James, Carol and Donna just look at each other. Finally, James and Donna both ask, "What the hell was that about?"

Carol just rolls her eyes. She knows what just happened, she wasn't born yesterday. James and Donna may not have picked up on it yet, but Carol is considerably older, smarter, and a little bit quicker than all they are. Although she would like to kill Anna, she finishes what James started to explain to Anna. "We have orders to look after you."

"You? What? You guys were trying to kill me. Now you have orders to look after me?"

"Yeah that's right. I know we've had our differences, but now that you got those hunters after you. We have to put out differences aside."

"Wait a minute, how did you know the vampire hunters were after me?

"Honey please. You're all over the News, I knew you were trouble, and I thought Donna was stupid."

"Carol, why do you have to be so mean to me?"

"I'm sorry Donna. I didn't mean to hurt your feelings, you know I love you, but boy do you goof up some times. Not like this one here, at least you're getting with the program. Anna fucked me and James up back at that alley, she tried to kill you. Besides, some of the things you use to do when you were with me, I had to wonder if you were trying to get us busted."

"Carol? Come on."

Carol gives Donna a big hug, and a kiss, which shocks the shit out of her. Carol let her go and playfully slapped her upside the back of her head. "Now cut it out okay? You got me looking gay out here." Donna just smiles, but at the same time she's still shocked and doesn't know what to think. Carol has Donna's head messed up for a minute. James laughs. He thinks they're a trip, if they had kissed a little longer it would have made his day. Anna is surprised was well.

"Wow, I didn't know y'all get down like that."

Carol looks at Anna and smiles, then punches her right

in the mouth. Anna falls flat on her back. People still out on the street witness this and can't help but to laugh, including James and Donna. Anna is so angry that she gets up and swings wildly, but she misses when Carol ducks. Carol knees Anna in the stomach, causing her to buckle. Then she tries to put Anna in a chokehold, but Anna flips her, then gives her an elbow on top of the head and kicks her in the face. When Carol falls backwards, Anna gives her a knee drop and then sits on top of Carol; her knee still pressed against her stomach and whales on Carol something fierce. The small crowd witnessing the fight is dumbstruck, including James and Donna. They decide it's time to break up the girl fight. They quickly pull Anna off of Carol. Donna holds Anna back, and James holds his girlfriend. Anna notices that Donna is a little bit stronger than Carol. Carol is kicking and screaming.

"James! Let me go. I'm going to kill that broad!"

"Woman, you need to chill. We didn't come here to fight her."

"You like her don't you? You're always sticking up for her,

and don't think I don't know about that night y'all went for that ride. What did y'all talk about? Huh?"

"Yeah it was a catastrophe. I bit her again, then she got insanely hungry and went to the supermarket."

"Oh Okay. Wait a minute. Did you like it? Yeah don't lie, and I know she liked it more. I bet she didn't even fight."

"Carol. You're in my arms and your acting like a crazy person, calm down."

"Okay okay." Carol takes a breath and cools off.

Two out of the three undercovers watching the front of Anna's home almost blow their cover watching Anna and Carol go at it. The two officers in the car are out and have run over to Anna during the fight, but since Anna's only fighting another female they're not quick to intervene. When Anna starts winning, they just watch. It's a good thing that those girls broke up their own fight, of course with the help of that James guy. But it's an even better thing that they were not the only ones running toward the fight. One of the undercovers looks at his watch and sees that it's ten minutes after midnight. This shift is going to be one wild and crazy night.

Donna has told James that she's hungry, which reminds Anna that she has a bag of blood in her car. She gets that big black bag, takes it in the house and puts it in the freezer. Donna says that she smells food. James asks Anna if they can come in and eat. Anna says hell no. James begs her, and then asks Carol to apologize. Carol looks at him like he's crazy before lightly kicking him in the butt. Anna thinks that's hilarious and laughs her butt off. Just like that, some of the ice is broken.

"Okay but I still have one question, who sent you guys here?"

James answers her. "Mrs. Page, Stephanie page."

"Huh? What? Did you just say Stephanie Page?"

"Yes, Stephanie Page."

"As in Dr. Page's wife?"

Then Carol answers:

"Yes, as in Dr. Aaron Page's wife. I didn't know that you knew the Pages. When she sent us to your address. I had explained that Donna and I had beef with you. She said to put our beef aside and help you out." Anna isn't sure she should believe what she's been told, especially coming from Carol, of all people. She has all three of them wait outside and calls Mrs. Page. It turns out that it's all true. Stephanie sent them to her house to protect her tonight and teach her the ropes about being a vampire. Apparently, Dr. Page forgot to mention this to her when she was picking up the pint bags.

Anna gets off the phone and invites them in to her apartment. Donna goes straight for Anna's freezer, and opened it, and before Anna says a word, James had reminds Donna to have some manners. Carol just sits down on the couch and chuckles.

"Anna can I have one?"

"Sure go ahead."

"Thank you."

Donna grabs three bags, and tries to grab a fourth, but Anna stops her. They end up splitting all twelve pint bags from the hospital. After their late supper, Carol explains a little about being a vampire, and a little extra she feels Anna needs to know. She explains everything that she told Donna about the origin of Mr. and Mrs. Page. She talks about herself, James, and Donna and why it's so important to keep the existence of vampires a strict secret at all cost.

"Wait a minute Carol, you're only 90, and Stephanie is 200?"

"Yup, I'm not old. Neither are the Pages. Aaron Page is only a couple years older than his wife. I think he's 202 or 203. He turned her shortly after he was bitten to save her from an illness that they had no cure for back then."

"So who are the oldest?"

"Oh that would be the council. They are the oldest of the elders, but before I talk about the council, I want to tell you about your elders. They too eat pint bags a lot of the time, that's because they have mortals who they trust. Well they don't really have to be powerful mortals; it just happens that way a lot of the time. However, usually only the elders and vampire soldiers are allowed to talk to the council. They are the big bosses, and they never deal with humans directly."

"Wow, this vampire stuff is big huh?"

"Yeah, they have an empire. I'm only familiar with the

council in Europe. Well I was told by the Pages. I heard there are other councils as well."

"Don't worry. I don't think you will ever meet them. Those are the bosses of the empire. The Pages are considered elders, and they are kind of powerful."

"So Carol, what do you know about the vampire hunters?"

"Oh them, they're mortals who know about us, and they hate us."

"So I saw, then I heard."

"Yeah they are sneaky and smart little people. In my opinion, the only thing keeping us from killing off those weak little cowards is that they are smart and sneaky."

"Where did they come from?"

"Do you ever watch TV? A lot of the stuff is true. You keep some things to secret, when anybody finds out about us, that's not good."

James leans forward. "Yeah I had to kill a couple of hunters myself. After that, a bunch of them got together to try to find who did it. Do you know that they even have cops on their team? But that's not all, they come as all kinds of people that you would least expect."

"Yeah Mrs. Page told me something about that, after she hung up on me when I told her that I was a police officer."

Carol continues, "oh, and we are not allowed to turn anyone without the permission of the council, or you can get in big trouble. If you bite someone, you have to kill them."

"Yes I have injured a female hunter, and licked some of her blood that was dripping from her arm. It was delicious, but then I noticed that she was wearing garlic on her neck, and it smelled awful. Then the sun got a little hotter and a whole lot brighter."

When Anna says this, Donna looks at James, James looks at Carol, and Carol looks at Anna. For a moment, there is a still silence. All eyes are now on Anna and nothing is said.

"Okay, why are y'all looking at me like that?"

"Um, Anna, are those pint bags the only thing that you have been eating for the past week and a half?"

"Yes that's it. What else would I eat? I'm a vampire?"

"Um, yeah you know what? I'm going to give you permission to drink from my man tonight, if that's okay with you James."

"Yeah it's okay, just don't take too much, or my girl is going to have to pull you off of me okay?"

"Thank you, but I don't do that, or at least, I'm trying not to."

Then all three of them trade looks again. First Donna speaks. "How can you stay eating those nasty donation bags?"

Carol narrows her eyes at Anna. "Oh I see what you're trying to do, you don't want to be a vampire and you think you're smart."

"What are you talking about? What do you mean I think I'm smart?"

"Lets just say that if anything happens to James, I will bury you if you turn mortal. If you stay vampire, than we were both wrong, but I will still get you. I will tell the Pages, and if they don't do anything, I'll find the council and let them know about you. How you refuse your gift of being an immortal. You don't want the council after you."

Now Anna is pissed off. She already knows Carol didn't like her, and respects it, but now this woman is crossing the line. She pulls her gun that she's been holding back ever since she got out of the car, presses it against Carol's head and yells, "Look you stupid old young lady, I'm sick and tired of your shit! Do you want me to bury you?

Carol is so shook that she ducks like a scared turtle, and the look that she gives Anna is priceless. Then James quickly speaks up. "Anna okay calm down, please don't do a thing like that!"

"Yeah, but I want to hear that plea from Carol."

"Anna come on, don't shoot my girl. She's a vampire. You know she won't die."

"Good, how would she like a three-day migraine? Three hours? I don't know. You want to find out?"

Carol's voice is frightened, but controlled. "Anna please don't shoot me." This cheers Anna up.

"Yeah, now that's a lot better."

Donna has been sitting on the couch, with her hands around her elbows. "Well, everybody, first of all, if Carol gets a hold of the council, we are all dead right? I mean, the Pages fled their country running from them, and none of us are suppose to be vampires, and Anna's all over the damn news. I don't think the council would even want to be bothered with us."

"Shut the hell up Donna."

"No I'm serious Carol. We're all knee-deep in shit now. If the council wants to kill us, then all they have to do is sit back and let the hunters do it."

James and Carol mull that over for a quick second, and realize that Donna is absolutely right. Donna may be a little inexperienced in the way of the vampire, but she isn't a stupid person, and she has plenty of common sense.

"Donna I'm sorry that I yelled at you and called you dumb blonde. I know you're not dumb; I'm just a hot head. Now Anna, let's try not to fight."

"Agreed."

"Wow, did you girls just have a spiritual awakening or what?" Then they all fall out laughing. "And Carol?"

"Yes James?"

"You should be a little nicer to Donna, before she kicks your butt too, again. I'm serious baby, you need get yourself into boxing or something."

"Donna is stronger than me, and Anna."

"Maybe so, but not by much, I thought Donna had the bad temper. I'm going to try to keep you girls from fighting so much."

The girls agree not to kill each other, and James suggests that they all go out to a bar. Anna isn't with it, but Carol says something that shocks the other three.

"Anna, you can come out with us if you like, just call your police friends who are outside and let them know that you're going out for a while."

James and Donna look bewildered, but Anna looks like a deer caught in the headlights: dumbstruck.

"The police are watching Ann's house?"

"Yeah they are. Anna are you okay?" Anna's speechless.

"Come on now, you know I know these things. I've been around long enough to know cop cars when I see them. Besides, those guys in that Ford, I noticed they were sitting there for a long time. It's 1:30 in the morning and they are probably in the car asleep right now."

Carol is on point. She's so sharp that she frightens Anna, until she remembers that she had told the Pages, who just might have told Carol. Donna puts a hand on Anna's arm.

"Come on Anna live a little. James and I forgive you, and so does Carol believe it or not. Beside, the Pages don't play. You got bigger problems than us right now, and if the Pages find out that we let something happen to you on our watch tonight, we will all be dead girls."

They all burst out laughing.

"Ha ha ha! That's not funny Donna, I'm not a girl."

"I know. That's why you're going to be the only one alive, you handsome smooth operator you. You'll probably charm Stephanie's socks off."

The girls laugh. Carol wants to laugh some more: " Hey Donna, tell us what he's going to say."

"Oh he's going to be calling Stephanie from a payphone, saying, 'okay um, please don't do a thing like that. Pretty lady don't shoot me please.' The girls almost cried laughing. James had to laugh too, Donna was on a roll.

"Come on Anna, I will treat you. Let's all get drunk."

"Okay why not, let's take my car."

The four of them drive to a bar up on the West Side and

had a good time. They don't stay late because James has some friends in the Bronx that he wants to see. Carol doesn't mind, Donna's just riding along, and Anna isn't sure if there's going to be a tomorrow. So they cruise to the Bronx and hit the bar that James says that some of his friends might be in. They aren't there, but that doesn't stop them from throwing themselves a party until 4:00 in the morning.

It's October 26, so the sun shouldn't be coming up for about another three hours. As they leave, Carol just asks Anna to drop them off in Ozone Park. Instead, Anna makes sure that she drops them off at their door, and that they go inside their apartment building before she drives off.

On the way back to her place she gets pulled over. The worst part about it is that she's drunk. She realizes that she can drink things other than blood. That's good news. "Wait, right now I'm pulled over and I'm drunk" she says to herself, as the policeman walks over.

"Hello Ma'am, can I see your driver's license and registration please?"

She just gives it to him without saying a word, and tries not to make eye contact as he takes her driver's license. He asks her if she knows why he pulled her over. She just shakes her head. So he tells her that she forgot to turn her headlights on. He runs her license and comes back. It doesn't take long at all. As soon as he sees that she's a cop he stops right there and comes back.

"Hey you're a police officer, why didn't you just show me your badge?"

Oh no, this means that she'll have to respond. She knows that if she opens her mouth he'll smell alcohol all over her breath. Now police officers give each other many passes, but many don't play that drunk driving stuff, even with other officers, and she's still in Queens. So when he hands her back the license, she turns her head toward the passenger side, as she put the license back in her purse. "Sorry about that, I had a long rough night."

"Yeah I understand. Well, have a nice day Officer Davis."

"Thank you. You too."

Then she starts her car as the officer walks away.

"Davis, don't forget your headlights!"

Anna smiles and waves, and turns on her headlights.

When she makes it back to her apartment in Manhattan, she parks her car and staggers into the building. Then she drunk dials the hospital because she's hungry again. "Hello is Mr. Page there?"

"No Ma'am, you mean Dr. Page? He left at 4:00, 40 minutes ago."

She hangs up, goes to the bathroom to hang over her toilet, and then takes a shower. When Anna gets out, she closes her bedroom door and jams it shut, then goes back to the couch in her living room, still made up as a bed, and gets in naked. She's out in a minute.

Back in Rhode Island, Tommy had wakes at 10:08 in the morning at his place. After brushing his teeth, washing his face, and getting dressed in some black sweat pants and the hood sweater, he calls seven of his 15 students who are also hunters, and puts them on stand-by. Then he calls Steven.

"Hey Steven this is Tommy. Are you ready for me to check out that vampire police chick from Manhattan?" He is hoping that he will say no, but he knows him, so he knows better.

"Yes I am. But first let me make a couple of phone calls, I'll call you back in a few."

"All right."

About ten minutes later Steven calls him back.

"Yeah Tommy this is me again. I heard that this Anna girl is under 24/7 police protection. A police lady from Providence is going to be calling you in about ten minutes. I want this vampire dead, but first we better figure out who all she knows, and see if she has any powerful connections, you know besides the police. They don't know anything."

"Yeah you're right. That's a good call. Now if something happens, how would I kill a vampire? A wooden stake thought the heart, or a cross-bow right?"

"Yeah that's right, but I wouldn't advise trying to stab a vampire with a stake while they're awake. They are much stronger than us. You know that."

"So my best bet, if they are awake, is to shoot them with

cross-bow?"

"Yeah. Oh, and the males are still stronger than the females. So if you're going to kill a male, you don't want to be alone. Now if you are alone, you want to use a gun."

"A gun? That doesn't kill vampire, does it?"

"It does if you use hollow tip bullets filled with garlic, or silver. But here's the thing, you have to hit them in the head or the heart."

"What happens if you hit them anywhere else?"

"Then you will hurt them, but you will also make them really angry, and they will kill you. Plus have you ever been shot at? You find strength and speed that you didn't know you had. Don't miss with a gun; you may activate or sharpen their survival skills and great speed. Besides, gunfire causes a scene, and scenes cause police. The biggest problem with that is, some of the police, as well as others, work for elder vampires. So use guns only as a last resort.

It gets a little deeper than that, but don't worry about that, stick to the basics, and you won't go wrong."

Now Tommy feels that he 's out of his depth for sure. Steven must have read his mind. "Oh and Tommy, I know this vampire hunting thing is new to you, but some of your men have experience killing them. You'll be fine. Besides, we're just spying on her for now. I will have my sister call you shortly."

"Okay, I got it."

Three minutes later, Tommy's phone rang again.

"Hi Tommy, my name is Officer Howard."

Oh shit! What the hell happened! Who is this lady officer? What does she want? If he would have looked at the caller ID and, wait police calls are private anyway.

"Officer Ashley Howard. Yeah my god-brother Steven gave me your number."

Oh yeah, damn. Tommy feels really stupid freaking out like that, and Steven had just told him that she would call in a few minutes.

"How are you Ms. Howard? I mean Officer Howard? Can I call you Ms. Howard?"

"Sure, I don't mind. I'm calling you from my cell phone. Yeah this vampire lady from Manhattan is being watched and protected by her fellow officers down there. Today, I'm supposed to go with you and help you bypass their officers."

"Thank you Ms. Howard. You have already helped a lot."

"You're welcome, and you can call me Ashley if you like. Ha, or if you meet my family, and just call Ms. Howard, then all the girls in my family are going to turn around to answer. Tommy laughs too. "I understand Ms. Ashley."

"Well, are you ready Tommy? If you give me your address I can come by."

Before he gives her his address, Tommy warns Ashley that he has seven men on stand-by, but she doesn't agree with that idea at all.

"So you plan to drive to Manhattan with two cars loaded with four men a piece?"

"Well yeah, why not?"

"Oh honey no-no-no, you're going to look like you're going on a drive by mission. You're going to get all kinds of attention, especially from that police woman's protection squad."

"Well what should I do?"

"Call six of your men back and tell them never mind, because you only need a small team. Then call the seventh guy and take him. After that, call three of the female hunters instead."

"Too many men huh?"

"Exactly, you and I are going to go down there as a couple, then there will be one more couple, and two home girls."

"Oh I get it! Ashley that is brilliant."

"Just glad I could help. They'll never see us coming."

Wow, Steven wasn't lying. Those Howards are brilliant. Tommy is starting to wonder why Steven left him Captain and third in command instead of one of them. Then Tommy proceeds to call his six hunters, and calls three female hunters and tells them to come over: it's time to hunt.

Ashley had shows up just a couple minutes later. Tommy hears the two light taps on her car horn, and goes ahead and opens the door. Ashley is beautiful. About 5 foot 7 inches, she has pretty brown eyes, and gorgeous dark brown hair and tanned skin. Tommy is star-struck and forgets to even say hello. Ashley smiles, then flicks her hair.

"Yeah, I get that a lot. You don't look bad yourself."

"Wow. So you're the youngest sister?"

"Yes I am. How did you know? Steven told you?"

"Yeah, I remember Steven telling me a little bit about how he grew up, and you're a year younger then Steven, 34?"

"My goodness you know a lot about me."

"It's not like that Ashley. I admire your whole family for taking Steven in."

"Wow, you look younger than 30, how old are you?"

"I'm 28. May I add, you don't look like you're in your 30s either?"

Then she smiles. "So Tommy, what else do you know about me?"

"No, Ms. Ashley I don't want to make you feel uncomfortable."

"Nope, tell me right now."

"Okay, you are Joe Howard's daughter right?"

"No, that's my Uncle. I'm Edwin's daughter."

"Oh okay. Well, I almost have a perfect memory. I don't mean to sound out of line but can I have a hug anyway?"

She puts on a serious face for a minute. "Tommy, yeah you're out of line. Do you think that you can just push up on me like that because you like and know a little bit about me?

"Wait, um, Ashley?"

"Huh? What?"

Tommy is so nervous that he starts stuttering as she charges him up.

"I would call that a bribe, what do you think?"

Tommy just puts his head down. Then she smiles and starts laughing.

"Boy where is my hug?" She gives him a warm hug and a kiss on the cheek.

"You know I was just messing with you right? Besides, you should have paid attention to Steven a little more. I love bribes." Oh this girl is a hand full, and boy does she have a sense of humor.

One of the hunter's pulls up, the guy that he called over. Tommy knows that it won't be long before the women show up. They sit and wait for them for 20 minutes. His crew arrived and gathered, Tommy explains the situation and what they're going to do.

"So we're just going to pair up and spy on her?"

"That's right, but only until we figure out who she knows, and who they are. Also, were going to figure out who this Anna girl is with, besides the police."

"So what should we do with the crossbows we have in the trunk?"

"I would say keep them in the trunk. We should be fine, what do you say, Ashley?"

"Well yeah you can keep the cross-bows in the trunk, as long as y'all don't have felony criminal records, and the arrows are not in the trunk as well."

Nick, the guy Tommy had called, has a drug and gun felony from getting into a shoot out on a drug deal gone bad in Western New York. He and a couple of guys were supposed to sell three kilos in Jamestown. The prosecution's case was shaky, but not so bad that he didn't decide to hedge his bets and take the plea deal for two years, instead of going to trial. He had to leave his crossbow with Tommy. One of the three ladies has a pistol permit and hollow tip filled with garlic, because it's much cheaper than silver. Lisa has a .32 caliber semi-automatic. Ashley laughs at her. "Who are you going to shoot with that? Rabbits?" Ashley laughs again before showing her police-issue .40 cal.

"Now some officers still carry 9mms, but this right here, will drop even a vampire, for a while. All I have to do is shoot him in the head."

"Okay? Then what?"

"Then I'll stab him in the heart with a stake."

"True, yeah that will work. You brought a stake?"

"No, but can I borrow one of yours?"

Then they all start laughing. They hit the road in pairs, two in each car, two couples and two female friends just hanging out. The time is 12:17pm. The three pairs are heading down to Manhattan. Steven has them fixed up in hotel rooms there for a couple of days, three rooms for $600, thanks to Dion Evans.

9

At 2 pm, Tommy decides that it's time to take a walk to Anna's block and look around. Ashley reminds him that they better check out Anna's watch dogs even harder. They go out two by two: Tommy with Ashley, Lisa with Amber, and Jamie paired up with Nick. At least one person has a cell phone in each pair so that they can keep in contact with each other while they walked in twos. Ashley and Tommy go first, because she has the best chance of spotting an undercover. Lisa and Amber walk across the street, a little behind them. Last are Nick and Jamie, who walk on the same side of the street as Tommy and Ashley, but far behind. They left the garlic, stakes, and crossbows in the car. The only two people strapped are Ashley and Lisa.

When they get to Anna's street, Tommy pulls out a

sheet of paper with the information that he wrote down about Anna. Ashley calls Lisa and Amber, then lets then sets up a three-way call. Nick has a smartphone, and he and Jamie pretend to look at something on the screen, while Lisa and Amber have earpieces. Tommy gives them Anna's address and description. Ashley keeps an eye out for the undercovers. She spots a man and a woman sitting in a gray Ford. "There's two of them," she thinks, but the hard part will be finding the other two, probably in a building watching from across the street somewhere, or perhaps standing around somewhere in the crowd, hard to tell. But for now, she'll tell the rest of her team what she knows.

After that, Ashley warns them that they should also walk around the corner to see who's watching the back of Anna's house. Tommy spots two men sitting in a Blue Infiniti, probably a seizure, and Ashley agrees. "Hey good eye. Yeah you're catching on fast."

"Yup, thank you."

Then they call the other hunters behind them, and let them know. When Tommy and Ashley walk past the back of

Anna's house, and up the street a little, Nick and Jamie see a man directly across the street from the back of Anna's place watching Ashley and Tommy. The guy in the house seems to have caught Tommy pointing at the undercover in the car, and Nick lets them know. So now it's known where all the undercover police are. The other cop has to be directly in front or Anna's house.

"Good looking. The guy who was watching me and Tommy, most likely thought that it was weird that he saw Tommy pointing out one of his officers, but at least we now know where he is, and whoever the person is on the other side. But he doesn't know about the rest of us, and that's if he even tagged us."

Then they turn the corner and got some subs at the sub shop. They make sure that they stay paired up, and away from each other. After an hour, Tommy has Nick and Jamie walk back around the block at the front of Anna's place, and he and Ashley walk around the other side to see if they're still sitting in the cars or standing around. Sure enough, the people they spotted before are the only ones in the crowd who are still there. Ashley and Tommy see the guy who noticed them the first time, and Ashley kisses Tommy. Tommy kisses her back and grabs her butt.

"Ha ha yeah, okay Tommy."

Then she smiles, and they walk by as a couple.

Lisa and Amber stay at the sub shop in case the other four get noticed, while Nick and Jamie find that two more assumed cops, watching the front of Anna's place. As they suspected, the other undercover cops are directly across the street from her on both sides. Now all they have to do was wait until 3:30pm for the next shift. That will be in 20 minutes. Ashley tells Tommy, and he uses her phone to let the team know. Then he calls Steven. "Yeah Steven this is me, Tommy. So far I've found out that there are police directly in front of Anna's house, front and back, there is a gray Ford with a man and a woman parked down the street watching the front, and two men in a Blue Ford down the opposite side watching the back. We are just waiting to see who shows up for the shift change."

"Good. So you've found all the locations of Manhattan's

finest?"

"Yes we did."

"And I know Ashley was a tremendous help?"

"We couldn't have done it without her."

Then Ashley wants to talk to him.

"Let me talk to Steven."

"Steven? Little Steven what's going on? You know Aunt Sallie said hi."

"Really? Okay, I'll call her in a few. Y'all got this mission on lock?"

"What? Who you talking to?"

"A Howard."

"And don't you forget it big brother. I got you're back. So what would you like us to do now?"

"Find out who Anna's been talking to."

"That's easy, what is her last name?"

"Davis, in the newspaper it says Anna Davis."

"Well I can pull up her phone record and have everyone she ever called."

"That good, really good. But the operator will look at us funny if I have my uncle do that, and you know they document that stuff?"

"No, we don't have to put him at risk of getting him in a jam like that."

"So. That's why she's going to do it."

"How is that going to happen?"

"Trust me. Just let me get her date of birth, her social security number, and maybe her mother's maiden name."

"I think I can get those for you. Call you back in a few."

"Wait, don't you want to talk to your captain for some guy talk. You know 'Hey Tommy, this is the general, kick down door, drag woman out by hair, and shoot anyone in the way.' Ha ha."

"You're I riot! I love you, little crazy sister!"

"And you know I love you too big bro. Now here's Tommy."

"Hey Tommy, I bet she's been driving you crazy, but listen to her, she's brilliant and she will keep you out of trouble."

"Oh yeah, I already know."

"Okay I'm going to get y'all that info on Anna, and I'll call you guys back."

A new set of undercover police show up for the shift change. Tommy and Ashley are hanging out at one of the restaurants pretending to have lunch out on the patio. They're already full, so Tommy orders the cheapest dish they have to offer, for the both of them. Nick and Jamie are doing the same. Five minutes after the new on-coming shift arrive, Tommy calls the teams, and they walk past the evening shift to get a better look at them. Lisa and Amber are getting bored. They even had to order extra subs, just to shut the employees up. But for now, they've got what they came for, and they catch two cabs, three by three, back to the hotel.

Steven calls on the way back in the cab, but Ashley doesn't want to talk in front of the driver. She calls him back from the hotel. He gives her Anna's first, middle and last name, date of birth, social security number, and her mother's maiden name. Then she remembers that all she needs now is the phone company that Anna's with, and her last address.

"Hold on, I'll have to call you back in a minute."

"Well Steven if you want, I can call Dion myself. "

Ashley calls her uncle, and gets the info. Twenty minutes later, Steven calls her back. He says that he heard that one of the undercover policemen had seen Tommy point out the undercover cop from last shift, but the guy didn't think that it was a big deal. "For a minute, the undercover was a little worried, but then he realized that he was just looking at a silly couple. So that means that you guys are good. Oh, I have the names of all the undercover police who are watching Anna if you want them."

"Okay thank you, but I don't think that I'll need them. Save it for me just in case."

"Sure, you got it." The time is 8 pm, and all the hunters on Tommy's small team have called it a night.

At 8:17pm, Anna has just woken up. She washes her face and goes to the hospital to get some pints from Doctor Page. When she comes back, she eats two bags, and puts the other bag in the freezer. She goes to visit her parents. They've kept in contact with Kyle, and some of the other police officers that Kyle has recommended. So when Anna arrives at the door she was surprised at what they knew.

"Pumpkin are you ok?"

"Yes. I know, I made the news again didn't I?"

"We didn't get it from TV this time. Honey you're all in the paper again. Are you Okay?"

"I'm okay, I just..."

"Yeah we know dear. Two men and a woman attacked you, but you shot all three of them, one is dead and another one died at the hospital right?"

"Yeah, all three of them are dead now. Kyle must have told you."

"Yes, but all it says in the paper is that you were attacked at you're place that morning. The names of the two men that were shot and the lady that they are claiming to have escaped the hospital. They didn't mention anything about the people being vampire hunters."

"I know mom, it's a secret organization. They are never going to mention it."

"Well Pumpkin, I and your mother have been talking to Kyle, and we thought that it would be a good idea to put you in the witness protection program tomorrow tonight. We already got everything set up."

"Really? Thank you. Where will I be moving?"

"Albany. Your friend Brenda said that people would never even think to look for you there. It's a good thing that she let us know that she stayed with you that night and you girls had protection."

"Whoa, Daddy! Brenda told y'all all that?"

"Yes Pumpkin, she told us."

"Donald, why are you giving up our sources?"

"Come on Carrie, Anna is going to find out sooner or later. Besides, we don't want her to think that we're spying on her. You taught me that a long time ago."

"Well Anna, I'm telling you right now, I'm your mother and I love you."

"Yeah Pumpkin and I'm your father, and we are going to

know the things you tell us, and the things you don't, any questions?"

"No daddy, and I love y'all too. I'm just surprised that Brenda told you so much. Wait a minute, I shouldn't be."

"Well Anna dear you should give Brenda a lot of credit, your father called her and got it out of her."

"Yeah Pumpkin, I got it out of her. It took me minutes and minutes but I did it."

Carrie Davis starts laughing her butt off. Then Donald finishes explaining.

"At first she wasn't going to tell your mother anything, but I explained to her that we are your parents and that we love you. Then I explained to her that we would eventually have heart attacks if we had to hear from the news first."

"That's right sweetie, so I hope you're not mad at her. Besides, your father always knew how to talk to the ladies."

Then they all laugh. Anna spends two more hours with her parents, before she calls Kyle at 12:30. Although she wakes him, he doesn't mind; the fact that she's coming over makes it better. She heads over there and gets her some, but she's a little upset because Kyle fell back to sleep. She uses Kyle's phone to check her answering machine. Brenda called her place at 11.

"Hey girl, it's me Brenda. Well I know that you're probably out right now, but call me back when you get in. Oh, and I have a cell phone now, so if you get this message after 11:30pm, just call my cell at..."

Then she read off the number. Anna calls her right back at 1:30am. She was asleep, but she doesn't mind. "It's ok I'm up know."

"I'm over at Kyle's place. He hit it and went to sleep girl."

"Ha ha ha, you put it on him huh? I knew you would."

"Yeah girl I guess, but I didn't mean to put him back to bed."

"Well girl, men are like that. Just snuggle up under him and get comfortable."

"You're right."

"Oh, I've been meaning to tell you, you're going to the witness protection program tomorrow night."

"I know, my parents told me."

Brenda paused. "Because Kyle told them."

"Oh yeah, so you're ahead of the game."

"No I lied, I know you told them." Brenda almost choked.

"But I'm not mad."

"Are you sure?"

"You did the right thing. I was too shook up and didn't think about it."

"Well they told me that they were getting worried sick about you. So I assured them that I too would look after you."

"Is anything else going on?"

"Well yes, Kyle said that your captain decided to give you an extra month paid vacation, and if you live through this, you're getting a promotion. So I'm kind of jealous, I just started working, and I can't see myself getting a vacation and a promotion at the same time."

"Wow, we all heard Kyle telling us about what the brass was thinking about when I was in the news. But they must have changed their minds. Kyle told them that you deserve a vacation and a promotion, if a street cop could deal with all of this and not go crazy. The Chief must have agreed. Kyle didn't tell you yet?"

"That is so cool. Wait a minute, Kyle, you and my parents all have each other's numbers?"

"Yes, we all got your back. Oh yeah I spoke with Julian, and she told me to tell you that she will be ready to come by tomorrow after school. But my suggestion to you is to go home and pack one change of clothes in a big purse or something and go back over Kyle's. Or come over to my apartment. Tomorrow night, you're leaving New York City until the smoke clears."

"Okay, but I don't want to be rude to Kyle."

"Girl, I don't think that he's going to be upset. Just make sure that you tell him that you're coming over to my place. He will probably say ok and go back to sleep." Anna pauses. Brenda adds, "Well you know he got to work in the morning anyway."

"Oh, yeah true. Brenda?"

"Yes?"

"You ain't never lied."

Anna asks Kyle if she can go over Brenda's to spend the night. She doesn't have to ask, but she does, and he says yes, no problem. Then Kyle throws on some slippers and walks her to the door. He is about to walk with her all the way down the stairs, but she gives him a kiss at the door, and says that she'll be fine. He looks at her, and sees that she isn't mad at him, he's feeling that it's some kind of test or something. "You sure?"

"Yeah I'm sure. Go to bed silly, I'm not going anywhere but over my girlfriend's place." Then she gives him another kiss and Kyle locks the door behind her. As she goes back to the car, she can just hear Brenda saying, "See? Didn't I tell you? He got to be at work in the morning." She stops at her place and gets two pints out of the freezer and eats a late night dinner, brushes her teeth, then grabs a change of clothes and drives over to Brenda's. She calls Brenda's cell before she leaves, and when Anna gets to her place they tiptoe past Brenda's mother's and little brother's room, and straight to hers. The time is 2:13am, and Brenda tries to stay up for a while, but falls asleep a half hour later. Anna takes it as a sign to chill and she falls asleep too.

Tommy wakes at 9:30am and watches the news. Nothing out of the ordinary. The maid knocks and wakes Ashley. She takes the old towels and washcloths, replaces soaps and refreshments. When she leaves, Ashley gets all of Anna's information down and calls Anna's phone company from a pay phone.

"Hell, my name is Anna Davis, and I need a copy of my phone record."

"Sure Ms. Davis, can I get your date of birth and the last four of your social?"

Ashley gives it to him, and everything else he asks her for. Then she asks him to mail it to her old address, which happens to be her parents' apartment.

"Sure I can do that Ms. Davis."

"Thank you. How long will it take for me to get it?"

"Oh, you will get it tomorrow morning."

"Thank you." Then she calls the post office, and finds out what time the mailman runs in that area. After that, she comes back to the hotel and calls the team to her room to let them know how things went. When the other four leave, it's just Tommy's and Ashley's. Tommy slaps her bottom.

"Good work for a bad girl."

"Hey look with your eyes, not with your hands. Man come on, I'm just kidding, I like you. If I pretend to be mad at you, you might never do that again."

"I'm not that scary, am I?"

Then she smiles and bends over so he can do it again. He does, he pops her booty, then he squeezes it.

"Hey mister, you can pop, but you can't squeeze."

Tommy is speechless.

"Yet."

Tommy knows what she's doing, he knows he's got her, and he just chill and talks to her. In fact, all of the hunters chill for the day, and the night.

Ashley's up the following day at 8:00 and wakes up Tommy to ask him to come with her to get Anna's mail. He agrees and also wakes everybody else to let them know, and to handle the hotel check out. Then Tommy rides with Ashley to the apartment building where she is be expecting the mail. When they get there, they talk about Plan B. "Okay captain, I'm going to wait in the building, and when the mailman comes, I'll get the mail."

"So what's the Plan B thing? If he doesn't give you the mail, what do you want me to do? Take it from him?"

"Well, yeah."

"What?"

"Come on Tommy, I got your back. He won't kick your ass."

"What?"

"Ha ha ha! Hey you know, if I end up having to whoop his ass for you, then you better not ever make me mad."

"What? I'm not going to get beat up, not by a mailman. It's just that Steven said that you were trying to keep me out of trouble."

"Oh honey, I am. Just stay out of the camera, and besides, that's only if plan A doesn't work. I'll do my best, but if I flick my hair, that means I need your help."

Then there's nothing to do but wait for the mailman. When they see him down the street, Ashley gets out and walks to the front door of the building. A lady who lives there used her opens the door and Ashley walks in as she walks out.

When the mailman comes to the building she greets him.

"Hello."

"Hi, how are you doing today Ma'am."

"Good. You got some mail for me today?"

"I don't know, what's your name?"

"Davis. Anna Davis?"

"Oh I see your last name on here."

Then he looks in his bag and gets a package.

"Here you go ma'am. Can I just see your ID, and can you sign this?"

"Oh sure you got a pen?" She takes his pen a signs.

"Wait a minute lady I have to see your ID."

"Oh sorry. Okay, honey I have to go upstairs and get it real quick."

She's seconds away from flicking her hair, but she remembers something.

"Would you like to come with me?"

"How many floors Ms. Davis? Oh, three?."

"Yeah, but the elevators are being worked on right now. You can just wait inside the hallway for me. I won't make you walk up all those stairs."

"You know what Ms. Davis? Don't worry about it. Here you go."

"Thank you."

"Oh you're welcome."

Then he gets back to work, and Ashley slides out the side door and motions for Tommy to come around with her car. He pulls around, and she gets in, and they drive off.

10

When they get back to Rhode Island, they all meet at Tommy's place to discuss how things are going and what to do next. Ashley's cell phone is dead, plus the two days are up and she has to get back home to her kids. But she stops by Tommy's real quick, and although she was to call her foster-brother and tell him how they did (or really, how she did) she lets him do the honors.

"Hey Tommy what's going on? Good news right?"

"That's right Steven, things went well. Your sister got the phone records for you."

"Really, how did she do that?"

"I think it was magic, Steven. Would you like to know what we got?"

"Yeah, tell me right now."

Ashley catches herself reaching for the phone, but Tommy doesn't see it.

"Well it wasn't easy, but we got the phone records of everybody that she called in the past year."

"Really? Give me the most recent."

"Okay this week, she called: Yvonne Greenmen, Donald Davis, Kyle Miller, Aaron Page, and the hospital. She of course also called the police station."

"That's pretty good Tommy, thank you, and tell Ashley I said the same."

Ashley can't take it anymore. She reaches and lightly takes the phone from Tommy's hand.

"Can I talk to him for a minute?"

Tommy just looks at her.

"Please?"

"Yeah go ahead, you already took the phone, you might as well"

"I didn't mean to be rude."

"You're okay."

"Hello."

"Ashley?"

"Yup I'm right here. Wow, 'tell me right now'?"

"Ah, you never miss a beat. Thank you Ashley."

"You're welcome, Little Steven."

"Come on now, only Aunt Sallie and Uncle Joe call me that. They almost had everybody calling me that."

"Ha ha ha, I know. But I'm not going to hold you up, I'll let you talk back with Tommy, I got to get back home to my kids. Hey, make sure you come by today."

"I will."

Tommy says he'll call back in a few, and they hang up. Ashley gives Tommy a hug and a kiss before she left. Then Tommy calls Steven back.

"Hey Steven it's me, I'm back. So what do you want me to do?"

"Well, first let me take a look at those phone records. Then I'll let you know what's next."

"Alright, I'll be there in a few."

"I'm not at home right now. But I'll call my wife and let her know that you're coming, so she doesn't leave before you get there."

"All right."

Then they both hung up. A minute later Tommy gets a call from Steven's wife to let him know that she's home. He delivers the records to Mrs. Evans.

A week later the hunters have done their investigations, and attack every vampire that Anna knows. Yvonne and Brenda Greenmen are neither attacked, nor harmed. But the hunters note the Brenda is a human, and Anna's best friend. Stephanie is attacked at her house in Long Island one night, while her husband is at work. The hunters, at the same time, attempt to kill Aaron at the hospital. He whips their butts, and they're forced to take drastic measures. They shoot him twice in the chest with garlic hollow tips, just inches from his heart. They try to shoot him in the head. On the third shot, he ducks and runs as fast as he can. Steven shoots him in the arm with a silver bullet and misses the other shot, as Aaron is smoking down the hallway. His speed is like nothing he could ever do before, and he's also forced to kill and feed on someone on the stairway while running up the stairs. Aaron also has to kill the second person on the stairway because he witnessed it, as he heads towards the roof so that he can building-hop in case they're still chasing him. But the hunters don't chase him very far.

They stop at the stairs. They can't catch him, plus they see that he's headed up; they figure it's better to just leave before they find themselves walking into a trap, plus the police and maybe even vampire reinforcement are coming.

At the house, eight hunters attack. They make four big mistakes. First, they've attacked a vampire at night where the grounds are even, two, they've attacked an elder who is faster, stronger, and smarter than the average vampire, and three, this one has servants and friends living with her and around her who she can trust, some of them are people she used to babysit. That brings it to number four, and probably the most important, she is not the only vampire in the house. Her friends Carol, James and Donna happen to be there at the time. Students of the Page's really, but they are here along with two servants.

This night, this fight, is one for the headlines. The hunters come three cars deep and they get out and walk along the driveway towards the Page Mansion. A small group goes around the right side of the house, past where Aaron's office juts out into a stand of pine trees. A neighbor has warned Ms. Page as soon as she saw strange men with crossbows. Stephanie grabs her shotgun, and gives Aaron's shotgun to James.

"The hunters are coming. Let's give them a nasty surprise."

Carol takes the liberty to grab Stephanie's handgun from out of the kitchen, and before Donna has a chance to ask for a gun, the hunters have kicked open the doors. As the heavy oak door bangs against the doorstop, Stephanie shoots the first man in. At almost the same time, they kick open the back door. James fires and blows another man away. Carol sticks her gun out the window, and opens up with the .38 special, and the hunters fall back. The vampire hunters find themselves hiding behind trees, cars, and the slope that leads down to the neighbor's house.

"Damn it! Vampires with guns! Why would vampires have guns?" one hunter yells, but only three hunters have firearms; the others have to make due with their crossbows.

It turns into a real western cowboys-and-Indians shoot out. On the second assault, the hunters gain a foothold in the foyer, one man putting his gun muzzle into the foyer and opening up cover fire while his comrades run into the wide hallway. Stephanie manages to take one out before diving around the corner into the dining room, just ahead of a burst of return fire.

The hunters hold the hallway while two go up to the bend in the curved staircase and take the high ground. Carol is forced out of the study in a rush to the right, and discovers that the hunters have the hallway when the door to the TV room is kicked in. She fires as she turns and misses wildly, takes a crossbow bolt with a silver tip in the right side of her chest. It knocks her on the floor and burns her to the point that she thinks she's going to die.

Fortunately, James has given up the back hallway and retreated through the kitchen. As he enters the interior hallway, two of the Pages' servants, great-grandchildren of their original servants, make a suicide charge from the second story, wielding antique floor lamps. With a couple of shots they go down hard, tumbling across the hardwood steps and spilling their improvised weapons onto the tile floor below. The distraction gives James just enough time to shatter the bones in the face of one hunter with the forehead of another. Then he twists the man's head around until the neck snaps. He gets two silver bullets in the chest, and one in the head. Out of ammunition and wounded, Carol crawls through the door to Aaron's office and pushes it shut. She weeps silently for herself, but also for James, and the life he could have had if he'd never met her.

Unarmed, Donna is forced to play hide and seek through the back rooms of the house, hoping to draw a hunter close enough to get her hands on him. Hiding behind a door to a pantry larger than her apartment, she hears one hunter give the order to "move out." The sound of gunfire continues from the front of the house, and she carefully makes her way forward, checking every corner for a man with a gun or crossbow. She makes it to the doorway of the dining room just in time to witness the final assault on Stephanie, as the surviving hunters close in and shoot her down. Her body bounces a little on floor and she turns to dust. The hunters turn and race out. Two cars waiting for them at the top of the driveway speed away before she has a chance to get a shot off with the gun she's picked up.

When the police come, they explain that they were attacked. They find out that the three men that were killed were from Rhode Island. The following morning, the vampire hunters are in Manhattan. They go to Anna's house and kick open the door, but she isn't there. Then they go to the police station to find Anna, Olivia and her fellow hunter who were missing, ready to do it at gunpoint if necessary. But they soon discovered that almost all of the police officers are gone, including Anna herself, and they don't have Olivia or her partner in custody. So they go back over to Anna's apartment. All her things are still there, so they figure she must have gone over to one of her friends' apartments, or a family member's. So they tap Donald Davis's telephone, and find that the Detective, Kyle Miller is her boyfriend. But they never mention anything about Anna's whereabouts over the phone. Surprisingly, neither does Brenda Greenmen.

Aaron Page gets some people and vampires together, to find out who the rest of those hunters were, and go after them. Then find out who sent them, and go after them, too. Carol on the other hand, goes out in a foolish blind rage. She goes to another elder she knows, and demands that he take her to the council. While she means no disrespect, she's out of line, but doesn't even care.

"Can you take me to the council? Do you know where they are?"

"The council? They don't know you. Are you crazy?"

"No! Well maybe so, but all I know is that that, the hunters have attacked us. Mrs. Page and my future husband is dead, I barely escaped with my life, and I don't know what to do, or who to do it to."

"Oh, I've heard about the attack on the Pages. That made headlines. The Pages fended them off well."

"Yeah I know, I was there! I caught an arrow in my chest. I got shot in the opposite side of where my heart is, and still almost died! Listen, I need you to take me to the council, and I need you to take me now!"

"Okay, calm down for a minute. So of course you know that Aaron got all of his people, vampire and humans together to find those guys?"

"Yeah that's true, but I have my own agenda. Besides, Aaron could use the help."

"They very well may kill Aaron."

"Then I will not let them know about Aaron, or anybody else except for the vampire Hunters in Rhode Island. Now that I think of it, there is one vampire I will have them kill, Anna Davis."

"Okay, I understand."

"Thank you."

"Yeah you're insane right now."

"Just! Can you just take me to the council please?"

"No! That's not smart."

"Then I will catch a plane and look for them myself."

"You wouldn't last two days."

"Well, I will do my best."

Then she walks off. He realizes that she is dead serious, and he doesn't want to let her go on a witch hunt, especially half cocked like this.

"Carol wait!"

"Yes?"

"If you are that determined to go, then I will escort you. Only elders and their soldiers can even come close."

"Thank you, Melvin."

He takes her with him to Spain, and Melvin rents a car and takes her to a strange house. He speaks to two vampire women and introduces them to Carol. Their husbands aren't home tonight but luckily for them, the two ladies are home, and know where and when the next council meeting will be, in four days. So they stayed until the husbands return. One of the men knew Melvin, and they let them stay. The man's name was Flexure, and he tells them that if they explain what happened back in America, then he would call the other elders, and they would have a meeting in two days. If they feel it's important enough, the elders will invite them to the council meeting a couple days later, and address the issue.

The elders' meeting is only seven people that day, but the idea of the council meeting consumes Carol. When they arrive, she is amazed and nervous at the same time. She has never seen so many vampires in one spot in her life. There are eight elite council members, all dressed as if they were still in the 18th century. Ho, they are sharp, but their fashion seems to be stuck in the wrong time. Then there are the elders, has to be about 16 of them; they wear whatever they want. Last, but not least, the soldiers, dressed in all black clothing, and carrying machine guns. Ten of them show up. Some time during the meeting, the elders who spoke with Melvin and Carol raise the issue about vampires getting attacked in America by vampire hunters.

"Who here is from the Americas?"

"A younger vampire named Carol. She wishes to speak to you."

"An elder name Melvin and a young lady named Carol sir? Carol wishes to speak?"

"Yes sir."

"Okay, then have her step forward."

"Yes sir."

Flexure and a couple others motion her forward, and she walks up front and center.

"Hello great men and woman of the council, my name is Carol Glen. I am here to inform you about the attack on us by the vampire hunter in America."

"The United States of North America right?"

"Yes that is right, the United States, in New York."

"Okay Ms. Glen what happened?"

She tells them, careful to leave out the names and address of the vampires that she was with.

"That's really quite bad, Ms. Glen."

"Um sir, you can just call me Carol if you like."

"And Carol, how old are you?"

"I'm 90."

"You're young. Who are you with? You never told us anything about your family."

She starts to get nervous, now that she knows that she can't mention the Pages.

"Um, the guys who attack us live somewhere in Rhode Island, in the northeastern United States. They killed my boyfriend, and I barely made it out alive."

"You're hiding something Carol, Carol Glen. How old was your boyfriend?"

"He was 43."

"That's a baby, who turned him? You?"

"Yes."

"You're not supposed to do that without our permission, or at least the permission of an elder. I'm assuming you took your own liberty? So I'll say he probably looked in his early mid 20's?"

"Yes sir, early 20's."

"Okay, we will take care of these vampire hunters, if you just lead the way, or point us in the right direction. So far we have your lead on Rhode Island, New York."

"Just Rhode Island. It's a separate state. It's about 180 miles or so."

"Yes sir that's right."

"Okay now we need the number your family's house, so that we may contact your elders."

"I'm sorry sir, but I can't do that."

"Excuse me?"

"I'm sorry sir, but I can't do that."

"Melvin. Are your Carol's direct elder?"

"No council, but she need to speak with you. It was very important."

"Yet, she can't tell me anything about her direct elder, or

family house."

"They were all killed sir."

"I'm sorry to hear that, but who were they? So we can know something about their background."

Melvin started to answer for her. It was clear that poor Carol needed guidance, in speaking with the council.

"Sir they were…"

Then Carol chimes right back in, cutting off Melvin in the middle of his answer.

"It doesn't matter, I came to you for help, and all you people care about is your old 18th century clothes, and who my family is, was."

The ancient vampire folds his fingers over the backs of his hands, staring at Carol.

"Young lady, do you realize that we could behead you for that?"

"I didn't mean any disrespect, but I just can't do the who's who right now, they not here. All that I care about is killing those vampire hunters. While I'm at it, we need to destroy a vampire by the name of Anna Davis, who lives in Manhattan.

If I could live long enough to see that, I will be happy."

www.ingramcontent.com/pod-product-compliance
Lightning Source LLC
Chambersburg PA
CBHW051445170526
45166CB00001B/120